NATURE BASED
LEADERSHIP

Lessons for Living, Learning, Serving, and Leading

STEPHEN B. JONES

LifeRich Publishing is a registered trademark of The Reader's Digest Association, Inc.

LifeRich Publishing books may be ordered through booksellers or by contacting:

LifeRich Publishing
1663 Liberty Drive
Bloomington, IN 47403
www.liferichpublishing.com
1 (888) 238-8637

ISBN: 978-1-4897-1095-6 (sc)
ISBN: 978-1-4897-1094-9 (e)

Print information available on the last page.

LifeRich Publishing rev. date: 12/19/2016

DEDICATION

I dedicate this book to three people who touched me deeply, all gone some twenty-plus years now.

Jack Jones, my dad, led me into nature and sowed seeds he never would have imagined could bloom and flourish in the manner they have. Dad knew and embraced the outdoors. "Nature based leadership" was not Dad's idea; rather, it is his inspiration.

Elmer Cessna, my father-in-law, believed in me, entrusted his daughter to me, and would have celebrated this book with pride and enthusiasm beyond what even Judy and I can muster. Elmer knew how to live, and he relished learning.

Zola Cessna, my mother-in-law, selflessly gave herself to all of us. She served with gusto, never seeming to worry about her own needs.

I miss them. A day does not pass without regretting that I did not devote more time and attention to them. I cannot even think of nature, learning, living, serving, and leading without seeing these three individuals surface through the words. I dedicate this book to them and the impression they left.

ACKNOWLEDGMENTS

Judy accompanied me on a hayride in October 1968. We dated steadily through June 1972, when we wed. We're still dating! She is the wind beneath my wings. There is nobody else with whom I'd rather share a sunrise ... or a sunset. She has encouraged my writing since long before I gained the courage to actually tackle this book.

I also acknowledge and thank Cheryl Charles for writing the foreword, and my dear friends and colleagues for their accompanying reflective essays: Craig Cassarino, Jennifer Wilhoit, Ron Dodson, and John Stanturf. Jennifer also performed superbly as my very first book editor—what a joy!

I also want to thank Matt Jones, our son, and Katy Disher, our daughter, for their love and the five grandchildren in aggregate they have brought into our lives: Hannah, Mallory, and Nathan (Matt's), and Jack and Sam (Katy's).

Because of friends and family, life is good!

FOREWORD

Imagine. Imagine a world of peace and beauty. Imagine a world in which children thrive; families connect deeply, playfully, and respectfully with one another; communities are vibrant, and the riches of the natural world are abundant and accessible to everyone. Imagine a world in which people *and* the planet are in good health. Imagine homes, neighborhoods, villages, towns, cities, and whole regions where nature is nearby, diverse, resilient, and beautiful. Imagine a planet where the semi-wild and wild places continue to nurture all of life, and the myriad species living together in communities continue to reproduce and flourish, while supporting all of the living world's inhabitants.

Imagining, creating, and caring for that world *is* the purpose of nature based leadership. Progress toward achieving that vision can be accomplished by doing what Steve Jones describes as seeing, feeling and acting while learning from, gaining inspiration from, and applying nature's lessons in every dimension of our lives.

I first met Steve in the spring of 2015. He was serving as President of Antioch University New England (AUNE) at that time, and had already named and created what he called the "Nature Based Leadership Institute," with its home at Antioch University. Steve had been thinking and talking about ideas related to the connections between learning and leadership, drawing on nature's lessons, for a long time—at least decades, if not in some ways from his earliest years. It was when he came to AUNE that the vision began to crystallize in new and compelling ways, in part inspired by Antioch's commitment to environmental, economic, and social justice.

While I had known of Antioch, and held it in high regard, I had never been to the New England campus. I had only met one of the AUNE faculty members, David Sobel, although I certainly knew of others by reputation and positive acclaim. David is a scholar, educator, leader, and visionary in nature based education. We are colleagues and friends with a shared interest in reconnecting children with nature for their health and well-being, and that of the earth itself. He is a key advisor to the non-profit organization, Children & Nature Network, that I founded with author Richard Louv and others in 2006. When I moved to New England, I had the opportunity to come to the Antioch campus to see David again in person. He said, "Let me introduce you to Steve Jones." At that initial meeting between the three of us in the spring of 2015, Steve talked about the Nature Based Leadership Institute.

Steve was authentic and compelling. I immediately connected with his vision and sincerity. Listening to him on that spring day, I said, "I have been inspired by nature based principles for decades and have put them to work in my own life—personally and professionally. I am explicit about what I call natural guides. If I can be of help as this new institute unfolds, I will be happy to do so."

Steve invited me to participate in the first of a series of planning meetings in which he was convening people from throughout the United States who he thought would have an affinity for nature based leadership, and who could make a contribution to the development of the Nature Based Leadership Institute. I participated in those meetings and was thrilled with the vision, passion, spirit, intellect, and commitment of all involved. Then, to my surprise a few months later, Steve asked if I might be willing to serve as the founding executive director of Antioch's Nature Based Leadership Institute. I have a history of founding projects and organizations, typically diving in for seven to ten years, and then handing them off to others to carry forward for the long term, while staying supportive and involved in various ways. This was a natural fit for me.

It is an honor to help bring this Nature Based Leadership Institute to life.

I offer here two examples of how nature based leadership principles have worked in my career. When I was the founding national director of the K-12 environment education program, Project WILD, we had annual coordinators' conferences. These events began in the 1980s and the state-level leads for this project, committed to integrating ecological concepts throughout mainstream education, came together to share insights, successes and challenges, and to get renewed. It was at these conferences that I first shared some natural guides to leadership that resonate with Steve's vision for how nature's lessons can guide us all. Diversity is the first one. Diversity tends to be an indicator of a healthy ecosystem. So ensuring there is variety among all of the people engaged in an endeavor, for example, allows for the stretching, growing, and nourishing of one another that lead to healthy outcomes. Connectedness is the second guide to leadership. We are all connected, in all that we are and do, so recognizing and cherishing those connections is a way to build bonds, strength, and resilience over time. The second example of nature based leadership principles at work in my professional life is on a larger scale. The Children & Nature Network that I co-founded with author Richard Louv and others in 2006 is dedicated to reconnecting children with nature worldwide. In my seven years as founding CEO, I continued to explicitly apply nature's lessons to help build this worldwide movement.

I share these professional examples to demonstrate that nature based principles *do* work. Project WILD continues to make positive contributions today—more than thirty years since its founding. The Children & Nature Network is also expanding and growing worldwide. Mine are just two examples of direct application of these concepts.

That leads us to today, and the important contribution that Steve Jones is making through this publication of his first essays about nature based leadership. Steve has a palpable, deep connection to the living world. As a child in Appalachia, getting outdoors was a way of life. It was also life giving and inspirational. With grit, effort, humility, and drive, Steve was the first in his immediate family to get a college education and graduate with a degree; earning his doctorate was unprecedented in his lineage.

What Steve offers us here is humility, insight, and awe. He guides us to look, see, and then to feel and act as each of us learns from and applies nature's lessons within our everyday lives. Steve says, "All lessons for living, learning, serving and leading are written indelibly *in* or powerfully inspired *by* nature." I believe in these lessons, and learn from my own experience of them every day—at home, in my family, in my work, and as a citizen of this planet. I hope each of you will do so as well.

Further, I urge you not only to read and incorporate these concepts into your own life, but also to share them with others. There are many people throughout the world who are seeing, feeling, and acting on this vision. Participate however and wherever you can. Reach out to connect with us and with others. Imagine a world in which each of us knows we are all connected, and each of us applies nature's lessons to all that we are and do. What will happen in the process? We, together, will be contributing to a healthy, thriving, and positive present and future for all, with nature as our guide.

Cheryl Charles, Ph.D.
Executive Director, Nature Based Leadership Institute
Antioch University New England

PREFACE

Forty-three years beyond earning a B.S. in forestry, I have come to believe that every lesson for living, learning, serving, and leading is either written indelibly *in* or compellingly inspired *by* nature. Over the past three years, colleagues (old and new) have encouraged me to further develop the concept, memorialize its precepts and tenets, and even create an academic core built upon nature based leadership (NBL). Several of us launched a still-emerging Nature Based Leadership Institute (NBLI) in 2015, based at Antioch University New England (AUNE).

My friends and colleagues inspired this first volume of NBL essays. Although a doctoral level scientist and university president, I refuse to write in academ-ese. Early in 2016, a scholar engaged in our NBLI conversations volunteered a definition of NBL that had many complex sentences nearly impossible to comprehend on the first read, and used words that are not common in everyday conversation.

The paragraph-long definition had a very low reading ease score on the Flesch-Kincaid scale, a standardized index to assess the accessibility of a piece of writing. The score suggests that understanding the text would require 10 1/2 years of formal education beyond high school. My own test is more qualitative. If I must read a sentence twice to comprehend, the writing is either too dense or the concept itself warrants more focused attention. If it takes me three or more times to get through a passage, I'm either too tired to read, or it is time to jettison the far-too-onerous writing.

Rather than crush the author's spirit by rejecting or, worse yet, marking up the text with red ink, I offered my own rewrite:

Nature based leadership (NBL) defines and elaborates an approach to leadership steeped in the ways of nature. NBL borrows lessons from the ageless evolution of individual species and communities. Far more species have failed than survived over the vast sweep of time. Individual species seek to reproduce, to carry the line forward, just as enterprises (i.e. a business or NGO) seek sustainability. Species employ adaptability, resilience, competition, specificity (such as niche exploitation), efficiency, reciprocity, and fecundity among many other strategies. Species often depend upon complex inter-relationships within the community (ecosystem) they occupy and, in part, compose. Each species has a plan, hard-wired in DNA. NBL identifies successful strategies and relationships, and extracts those that translate to enterprise applications that leaders can apply. NBL also leans heavily on nature's beauty, awe, wonder, and inspiration. NBL embraces tenets that can sustain the individual enterprise and assure Earth stewardship and human well-being. NBL both implores and enables us to care for our common home and our fellow travelers. (The Flesch-Kincaid reading ease on this passage is at a 12th grade level.)

Admittedly, my text is longer. However, I'll take simple and longer every time over near-incomprehensible. I also strive to make my essays entertaining, provocative, and inspiring.

The first essay in this volume begins a chronology describing NBL's evolution from vague concept, to the Institute, to this volume. October 2013 stands as the first formal benchmark, when I delivered the Fall Speaker Series at Antioch University New England, introducing my thinking about the nature of leadership. Nearly a year later found me delivering the Fall Convocation at Lapland University in Rovaniemi,

Finland, at the invitation of U. of Lapland rector and dear friend Dr. Mauri Yla Kotola. As I noted in closing the second essay:

> I had not yet in fall 2014 framed my message in terms of nature based leadership. Yet elements of NBL wove through those remarks.

By the third essay here, I had fully developed the idea and we had launched the Institute. I still pondered to what extent the NBL concept held merit. Was it simply some self-serving manifestation of my own passion for nature? As the essay title poses, "Is Nature Based Leadership Real?"

Having convinced myself that NBL is real, I then addressed the question of who might care about NBL. During the seemingly endless early 2016 Republican presidential primaries, I gave eight of the emerging NBL essays to my ninety-one-year-old mother, who read them with no apparent inspiration or enthusiasm. Crushed (and subsequently buoyed), I asked "Who Cares about NBL?" in the fourth essay.

The fifth essay, "Little Green Heron," shifts gears to reflect upon NBL from the perspective of a poignant experience during my adolescent youth. One fateful day, I had carelessly slung a rock toward a beautiful little green heron that, shockingly, hit the bird; this memory has occasionally surfaced over the intervening four decades. The incident made my list of nearly-fifty lifetime regrets.

My life and its journey toward fashioning NBL involved powerful molding and shaping. Some occurred through woeful incidents like the deadly rock. Others derived from the people I have been honored and privileged to know along the way. My sixth essay, "Jack Berglund's Belief in Me," examines one such relationship. Although Jack and I never spoke in even vague terms about NBL, he played a part in sculpting the fledgling scientist and young professional who would eventually envision nature as a force in understanding more clearly and compellingly how we can better live, learn, serve, and lead in all facets of life.

My compatriot NBLI founders (and co-conspirators) serve as scientists, practitioners, scholars, deep thinkers, and academics who not only assisted in creating NBLI but who are engaged in developing its programs, workshops, certificates, and degrees. I characterize my role more as the NBL poet. I am driven by nature's inspiration. Others can write about the hard and empirical elements of NBL. The seventh essay, "Snow in the Arc Light," digs deeply into the lyrical and metaphorical elements of nature's inspiration for living, learning, serving, and leading. I introduce the concept of nature's pleasurable terror. I close that essay reflecting on the title experience and contemplating the role my late father played in leading me to conceive, embrace, and proselytize NBL.

Benign nature likewise offers lessons. I am guessing that those who have been led to read this book are the kind of people who have seen dew-bejeweled orb weaver spider webs on a late summer morning. Again, I employ poetry (not real verse and cadence, but a more metaphorical poetry) in essays eight and nine. Both offer web-inspired lessons separated by several years and location; one occurs in Ohio and the other in New Hampshire. These two essays revolve around seeing the invisible–in things, in people, in opportunities, in potential.

The tenth essay in this book leads back into the teeth of pleasurable terror, specifically that which is induced by extreme weather. It demonstrates my passion for wild weather, and my ongoing and relentless search for lessons in nature, whether wild or benign. My "Winter Mount Washington Summit Attempt" (February 2015) draws deep lessons from experiencing nature in full frontal fashion. Even in *failing*, lessons, inspiration, and fulfillment are at hand. The following March I wrote the next piece, "Successful Mount Washington Winter Ascent." This eleventh essay tells of a less harrowing adventure, yet one that still draws power, passion, and inspiration from nature.

Second to last, I offer a piece that draws from my formal training as a forester and soil scientist. *Soil* is both physical substrate and the metaphorical medium that nourishes our living, learning, serving, and leading. Finally, this book concludes with the tale of "The Peregrine Falcon." I express in this thirteenth essay my abiding gratitude for nature as a "portal," a place that nurtures and offers solace, a locus for learning and reflection, a site in which my vision becomes clearer.

So much of my nature based leadership discovery journey emerged from interactions with incredible people I've meant along the way. As I prepared this first volume of essays, I realized that my writing alone might not capture enough of the purpose and passion that drive and inspire me. I asked four others who share my lifelong love of nature to add their own reflections on the subject. Their writing illuminates some of the corners that my own light may not reach. I am grateful for their words, support, and stimulation. I'm pleased that Ron Dodson, John Stanturf, Craig Cassarino, and Jennifer Wilhoit agreed to write guest essays. Their belief in the wisdom and power of nature serves as wind in my sails. I've known Ron for twenty years, and John since my PhD research in northwest Pennsylvania and southwest New York in the mid-80s. Craig and Jennifer have shared life's pathway with me for only a little more than a year, yet they have already enriched my journey.

I hope that reading these essays offers enjoyment, as well as an opportunity for contemplation on their essence and relevance. I relished writing them. May the seeds of nature based leadership find fertile soil, germinate, secure favorable purchase, grow, flourish, multiply, and motivate each and all of us to better steward our one Earth.

CHAPTER ONE

Nature Based Leadership: Conceptual Framework

I n October 2013 I delivered an address at the Antioch University New England Fall Speaker Series. My topic was entitled, "The Nature of Leadership," a theme I had been exploring for months. Over the course of 2014, I continued to develop my ideas and began talking to associates about where the theme could lead. We even established a working moniker for an International Academy for Sustainability Leadership. We could not find traction around that particular theme. I believe that the term "sustainability" suffered over-use fatigue nationally as well as internationally.

The "Nature of Leadership" returned to me time and again, leading me to the Concept Paper I present below in its entirety. Importantly, the concept has evolved only modestly since then. The Nature of Leadership shifted to Nature Based Leadership. And the construct moniker Center for Nature Based Leadership morphed to Nature Based Leadership Institute. The NBLI Founders and Executive Director Dr. Cheryl Charles will continue to develop, refine, and improve the concept. I offer this January 2015 document as a frame of reference, a starting point for all that followed and is yet to come.

Abstract

Eighteenth Century Swedish mystic, philosopher, theologian, and scientist Emanuel Swedenborg (1688-1772) adopted a central philosophical tenet—that the entire natural world comprises a series of physical symbols for a deeper spiritual reality. That is, nature embodies all lessons of life's physical and spiritual essence. I will explore reflections on how, likewise, our natural world offers powerful truths applicable to learning, living, and leading. I have found inspiration, solace, and illumination in the natural world, written more indelibly, powerfully, and succinctly than any management text could possibly encapsulate. Thus, I present *The Nature of Leadership* conceptually, and propose creating a Center for Nature Based Leadership.

Introduction

Swedenborg believed that *coincidence*, the seeming harmonic alignment of happenings in space and time, occurs only with purpose, meaning, and intent. That is, what we often refer to as *coincidence* is actually *correspondence*. I will speak to how such *correspondence* led me uncannily to this Antioch University New England presidency, and to link "leadership" more concretely to our natural world.

I begin with a single example of remarkable alignment: Urbana University, which I led for the five years prior to my AUNE role, originated in 1850 as a Swedenborgian University. That I would lead a Swedenborgian institution rises to the level of *correspondence*. I will explain.

True to Swedenborgian doctrine, I believe that nature's lessons apply broadly to life, work, and play. *Natural* leadership borrows tenets, principles, and relationships embodied in ecosystem patterns and processes that have operated since life first emerged from the primordial soup. This concept paper presents the nascent study and practice of nature based leadership. Encompassing a term appearing increasingly in both scientific outlets and common media, I propose applying the lessons of *biomimicry* to the art and science of leadership.

I have been the president of Antioch University New England since July 1, 2013. AUNE is a small, niche, graduate university (1,000 students: 1/3 doctoral and 2/3 master's), one of five campuses of Antioch University (based in Ohio). This is my third university presidency [Urbana University and University of Alaska Fairbanks (UAF)]. My AUNE budget is one-thirtieth the size of UAF's. Our AUNE "campus" is a single building—a repurposed late nineteenth century furniture factory. My eighth university, this is my smallest. However, this is clearly my BIGGEST job! So much is at stake at this institution which is superlatively purpose-driven and passion-fueled. Horace Mann, Antioch's founding president (1852) said to the first graduating class in Yellow Springs, Ohio, "Be ashamed to die until you have won some victory for humanity!"

With their median age at thirty-five years, our students and alumni really are changing the world. It's why students enroll. We can't let them down—again, the stakes for tomorrow's world are too high. It's why I'm here. And why this is my biggest job! Although this is my smallest university, this is not an easier assignment. Regardless of the stakes, this is my most comfortable leadership role. This is where I belong. This is where I comfortably apply the lessons of "natural leadership." There could be no better, more natural fit for me. This presidency is a perfect base for me to probe the depths of The Nature of Leadership.

This concept paper on The Nature of Leadership presents five elements:

- Context—my own lifelong passion for Nature
- Relevance of Emanuel Swedenborg
- *Correspondence* in my life/career
- Six Lessons in Leadership from Nature
- Creating a Center for Nature Based Leadership

Lifelong Passion for Nature

My maternal grandmother introduced me to nature through her flower gardens. Under her tutelage, I learned and appreciated the old standards: petunia, zinnia, marigold, four o'clock, cleome, snapdragon. My mother worked with me as I collected seeds from Grandma's plantings and sowed them late winter indoors for spring out-planting. Mom occasionally presented me with the pre-packaged starter boxes that required only punching holes in the covering plastic, watering as needed, and placing on an indoor windowsill. I still recall the thrill of seed-germination, the magic of seedling elongation, and the joy of transplanting outside. My reward proved both visual and tactile, with hands in the soil, nurturing and cultivating the live, growing product of my care. I thrill yet today some six decades hence as I tend our perennial gardens.

My dad immersed our family in the natural world via picnicking, hiking, camping, hunting, and fishing. Without realizing it, I was learning the lessons and wonder of nature. I was stocking the mental library references that I turn to now as I reflect more and more on The Nature of Leadership.

That set of experiences instilled an abiding love of forests, mountains and rivers, sunrises and sunsets, seasons, storms, patterns, processes, nature's beauty, power, fury, and places and maps. I am a creature and product of those formative experiences.

Relevance of Emanuel Swedenborg

Eighteenth century Swedish scientist, theologian, mystic, and philosopher Emanuel Swedenborg (1688-1772) wrote an exhaustive nineteen-volume set interpreting the Bible. Followers of the Swedenborg philosophy established the Swedenborgian Church (the New Church movement) in 1787. Famous Swedenborgs include Helen Keller, Andrew Carnegie, and John Chapman (also known as "Johnny Appleseed"). Robert Frost grew up a Swedenborg.

Relevant tenets of Swedenborg and the New Church include the following:

- A central philosophical underpinning is that the entire natural world represents a series of physical symbols for a deeper spiritual reality.
- Nature embodies all lessons of life's physical and spiritual essence.
- The term *correspondence* holds Divine Providence as universal, existing in every least thing.
- "Coincidence," the seeming harmonic alignment of happenings in space and time, occurs only with: purpose, meaning, implied intent. Nothing is accidental.
- "Coincidence" is actually "correspondence."

Correspondence in My Life and Career

I must ask, is correspondence real... or "just coincidence"? I don't know for sure. However, my life and career seem to have taken a route (an amazing route) that I could not have imagined, designed, dared, or repeated. Has anybody ever said to you, "Oh, if only I were twenty again!"? I don't want to see twenty again! Robert Frost observed in "The Road Not Taken": "Two roads diverged in a yellow wood..." and "Oh, I kept the first for another day! Yet knowing that way leads on to way, I doubted if I should ever come back." Way has provided well for me. I would not care to trust a repeat performance. Another choice? A different path? No, given another chance (to be twenty again), I could only choose less fortuitously, less serendipitously. I don't want to risk another chance!

Given another chance, how could I possibly repeat the good fortunes of people, place, and time that led me here? I offer three such uncanny alignments (coincidence or correspondence?). Each of these examples in my life and career truly evidences such correspondence.

I completed a two-year forestry program that had started the fall after my high school graduation, right in my hometown (Cumberland, Maryland) in Central Appalachia. I was a first-in-the-family college attendee. My family could offer no financial support to begin my forestry studies at a four-year institution. Maryland had no public university offering a bachelor's degree in that field. Coincidence or correspondence?

The founding director of the community college forestry program, a West Virginia University (WVU) doctoral graduate, modeled the new program after the WVU forestry bachelor's degree, and he worked closely in doing so with folks at WVU's forestry school. When the time approached for me to transfer into the WVU forestry program as a junior, that university reneged on the negotiated agreement, refusing to accept my full credit load. The founding director stood on principle, finding instead, in the SUNY College of Environmental Science and Forestry, an esteemed institution willing to accept all of my Allegany Community College credits. Way changed to way and altered the course of my life and career in ways I cannot fathom. Correspondence?

As a certifiable introvert, I entered forestry school, in part, because I loved nature and had no inclination to work with people. One of my professorial mentors/heroes at SUNY ESF had spent sixteen years in Franklin, Virginia with Union Camp Corporation (UCC), a multi-national Paper and Allied Products Manufacturing firm with forest-based operations in Virginia, North and South Carolina, Georgia, Florida, and Alabama. When he learned that UCC recruiters were coming to SUNY ESF to interview Paper Science Engineering soon-to-be graduates, he pulled some strings to have them meet this impending Forestry graduate. The net result? The company invited me to a formal interview onsite in Franklin, Virginia. After a day's interaction with Woodlands Division personnel, the Director of Community Relations (a unit that dealt with people!) met Judy (my wife since June 1972) for dinner prior to our next morning return flight to Syracuse. That evening Chris said to us, "Steve, if the folks in Woodlands do not offer you that position, I have a job for you in Community Relations." I wondered if he had confused me with another person! Instead, he had seen in me qualities and abilities I never knew were there. He saw deeply into my future. He planted a seed of realization and belief that has since flourished. Woodlands offered the forestry job and I accepted. If instead, Frost's "way" had led us to Community Relations, where would we be today?

So, was all that serendipity and fortuity—or, correspondence? Each step brought me closer to AUNE, where I belong at this stage of life and career.

Allow me now to shift back to Emanuel Swedenborg. In July 2008, I found myself the president of Urbana University (UU), a small, private liberal arts institution in west-central Ohio. As an invited applicant for president, I had never heard of the New Church, Emanuel Swedenborg, or Urbana University—founded in 1850 as the nation's first Swedenborgian University. I had served previously at only large public universities, yet there I was, responding to an invitation that I apply for the UU presidency. Imagine my surprise when I discovered that Johnny Appleseed, a devout Swedenborgian, had enabled the original gift of land for establishing UU. Contrary to Johnny's general reputation as a resolute conservationist, Appleseed actually performed as an "accidental" conservationist. He was first and foremost a Swedenborgian missionary, supporting his mission work by collecting apple seeds from western Pennsylvania cider presses, trekking west with bags of seed into the frontier, and cultivating seedling nurseries in Ohio in advance of the first serious waves of settlers. He sold or bartered seedlings to settlers, generating the means to fund his mission work.

The "correspondence" is uncanny. In 2008 I was the nation's only forestry-trained university president leading a university enabled, in some real measure, by Johnny Appleseed! Not only that, but I learned that the basic philosophy and tenets of the Swedenborgian faith were in alignment with my own belief that the natural world offers powerful truths applicable to learning, living, and leading. I discovered full alignment along multiple fronts. I find inspiration, solace, and illumination in the natural world. I have believed for some time that the lessons of leadership and life are written in nature more powerfully and succinctly than any management text could possibly encapsulate. Without the UU Presidency and its extraordinary platform for personal and professional growth (a private university in severe fiscal peril), I would not be here at AUNE.

I went to UU thinking it would be my last position before retirement. But May 3, 2012 changed that. While completing an after dinner walk within a block of our home, Judy and I were midstreet at a crossing when the driver (with revoked license) of a two-ton SUV (with invalid tags) ran a stop sign, plowing into us. The driver threw it into reverse and exited the scene with tires squealing. The impact sent us flying tens of feet. We were soon headed toward the hospital in dueling ambulances. Later, after we recovered, a neighbor who had been mowing her lawn and glanced up when we were airborne observed, "You were caught by angels." Bernard Malamud, author of "The Natural," spoke through his lead character, "We have two lives to live; the life we learn with and the life we live after that." This is our "second" life, spawned by the deep wisdom of reflection and introspection during recovery. This new, second life is more purpose-driven and passion-fueled—clearly, a *calling.* Antioch University New England called and we responded. We consider SUV-induced transformation as just another "correspondence."

Lessons of Leadership in Nature

These are not the "Six Lessons of Leadership in Nature," but simply six powerful examples. I could have chosen many more. This concept paper sets the stage and this set of examples is just a beginning.

Lesson 1: The complementary forces of humility and inspiration.

I offer a firsthand metaphor for learning, living, and leading. The University of Alaska Fairbanks sits on a bluff overlooking the broad Tanana River valley, stretching to the central Alaska Range some seventy miles to the south. The range extends west from there another hundred and twenty-five miles to Denali (Mount McKinley), North America's tallest at 20,237 feet, high enough to remain cloud-capped much of the time. Only occasionally could we see it from campus, appearing far to our southwest. We moved to UAF in late June and by mid-August we had still not seen the peak. We had guests coming from the East Coast and had planned a special treat. We drove to the entrance of Denali National Park, hopped into a friend's single engine plane that evening, and flew to Kantishna, a gravel airstrip on the north side of Denali, ninety miles beyond the park's entrance. We enjoyed great views of the park and clearly saw and appreciated the lower flanks of the mountain during the flight. We overnighted at the lodge near the airstrip.

I awoke early, hoping for clear skies, and was pleased to see no clouds. From the lodge and airstrip Denali hides behind 3,000 foot Mt. Quigley. I would need to climb Quigley to see whether the mountain would present a view. We grabbed a quick breakfast and headed out to the Quigley trail head, ascending Quigley's north shoulder. My eagerness spurred me upward, outpacing my colleagues who eventually turned back to the lodge. That countryside is all above timberline, offering clear views to the plains stretching without end to the north. I occasionally glanced back toward the airstrip, watching it shrink to miniature status. I felt smug, full of myself. Here I was climbing Quigley, trekking into the heavens, commanding a very impressive viewscape. Quite an accomplishment, I thought! As the trail began to flatten near the summit, watching my feet to secure firm footing on the cobbled surface, I felt a strange sensation, as though someone were watching.

Not realizing I now had a full view to the south, I stopped, turning my attention in that direction. My heart pounding, I saw only gleaming white with my level gaze. My eyes slowly following that white wall upward, my head tilting ever more toward the vertical, there stood the most magnificent sight of my life, before or since. McKinley rose 18,000 feet from the valley in front of me to its summit. Three and a half vertical miles of rock, glaciers, and glory towered in the late morning sun.

Stunned, I felt two emotions. The first was total humility. In a few seconds, I had gone from the arrogant satisfaction of climbing Quigley to the full realization that I had done nothing. Along with humility, I felt absolute inspiration. I stood before "The Mountain," grasping slowly what might be…, what could be…, what perhaps lies ahead… I felt inspiration to reach beyond my grasp, to celebrate every accomplishment. But also to know that always more lies ahead.

No, I will never summit McKinley. I will continue climbing mountains, metaphorically. I will embrace humility and seek inspiration. Humility and inspiration—try leading without them!

<u>Lesson 2</u>: Learning to read the lessons of the seasons.

Here in New Hampshire we annually live in the midst of Autumn Glory. Tourists visit from all over the world to view the spectacular result of a simple natural process. Trees translocate manufactured sugars from the leafy canopy to winter storage in the roots, leaving behind the colorful pigments. The aggregate rich colors carpet our hills and mountains, beckoning to all who might enjoy nature's palette. This transition season effect brings to mind Ecclesiastes 3:1-8, paraphrased as: To every thing there is a season, and a time to every purpose under heaven—a time to be born, and a time to die; a time to sow, and a time to reap.

The words reach beyond the meteorological seasons, expressing a truism that, indeed, applies to every "thing"! Every life, business, enterprise, position, program, career has its own seasons. These are emblematic seasons that portend, that signal change, and that call for preparation and action. Imagine a leader who cannot sense, appreciate, and understand the lessons written in the seasonal cycles in all endeavors—in everything!

<u>Lesson 3</u>: Knowing our place in the world.

Robert Service, a British poet, storyteller, and balladeer who spent several years in the Yukon gold fields at the turn of the twentieth century, offers a powerful metaphor for living and leading in his poem, "Security," which I recommend you find and read. Service introduces a limpet somewhat unhappy with her lot in life. The limpet is a creature of the intertidal zone, anchored to rocks to enable feeding as the tidal ebb and flow deliver nutrient- and microorganism-rich waters for filtering and feeding. The ribald sea offers the limpet a chance to cast off on the tide to free herself from the rock that clings to her so tightly.

The ballad continues as the limpet takes advantage of the sea's offer, beginning a perilous and frightening journey "on the laughing sea." Eventually, through several stanzas of treacherous adventure, the sea delivers our limpet friend to the sandy beach, where she may find safety and security. But the limpet begins with a sense of woe to realize that a limpet's lot is to cling. She cannot find purchase on the sandy beach. Desperate and suffocating, she hitches a ride with a "taxi-crab," who insists that she ride inside, thus meeting her fate. Service closes with:

> So if of the limpet breed ye be,
> Beware of life's brutal shock;
> Don't take the chance of the changing sea,
> But—cling like hell to your rock.

"Security" is a parable—a lesson for life, infinite in its application. Try leading without knowing your place and recognizing your anchorage, your own rock. Try managing and inspiring without appreciating what is critical, what is reality, and what is unchangeable. Rocks come in the form of ethics, character, integrity, fidelity to truth, and all else that constitute the higher road.

Lesson 4: Understanding limitations and potential.

I draw this lesson from my doctoral research, a field-research based examination of the relationships between key soil-site variables (direction of exposure or aspect, slope steepness, slope position, slope shape, soil depth, and others) and forest productivity in the Allegheny hardwood region of northwestern Pennsylvania and southwestern New

York. If a forest finds itself on a west-facing, convex upper slope, forget about high productivity! At the other extreme, a forest on an east-facing, concave lower slope can perform superbly. Soil-site conditions establish environmental potential. Although individual species' adaptability varies across site conditions, the site itself places absolute limits on potential.

Now, try leading without knowing both limitations and potential— of people, organizations, and operating environments.

Lesson 5: Knowing your own purpose in life.

In John Maxwell's "Daily Reader" I read: "A friend of the poet Henry Wadsworth Longfellow asked the secret of his continued interest in life. Pointing to a nearby apple tree, Longfellow said, 'the purpose of that apple tree is to grow a little new wood each year. That is what I plan to do.'" The friend would have found a similar sentiment in one of Longfellow's poems: "Not enjoyment and not sorrow, is our destined end or way; but to act that each tomorrow finds us further than today."

Imagine leading without knowing what motivates and fuels us, what enables and encourages us to add a little wood each year.

Lesson 6: Understanding and appreciating the perspectives of others.

Traveling along New England's winter roads, I often see resident hawks (very often red-tailed) perched on trees and utility poles, where fields and grassy rights of way provide perfect habitat for rodents and clear hunting for these magnificent birds of prey. I marvel at these incredible hunters. My mental lens characterizes the birds as beautiful, fearless, noble, regal, capable of effortless (and enviable) soaring, and as symbols of enduring freedom. How different it is through the eyes of a foraging mouse! The rodent appreciates none of what I see. To the mouse, the hawk is threatening, dangerous, preying, stalking, ruthless, diving, and a symbol of death. It's the same bird, yet each characterization is real to the observer.

Also, think about New England's forests through two human lenses separated by four centuries. The Old World's early colonists found the forested landscape dark and foreboding, foul and repugnant, evil, disease-infested, and home to savages. Today, we see woods of wonder (e.g., autumn's splendor), an escape from our work lives, a destination and not an obstacle, a place to reflect and renew, and as a source of solace and comfort.

An absolute truth in business, life, and politics—just as in nature—is that where you stand depends upon where you sit. Or, where you fall in the food chain. Try being a leader without knowing and respecting where others sit. Know where you fall in life's food chain!

Some Final Reflections: Toward Creating a Center for Nature Based Leadership

"The Nature of Leadership" is a relatively new (1998) and unique kind of business book. It contains exquisite photos by Dewitt Jones, combined with inspiring interviews, quotes, and narratives compiled by bestselling authors Dr. Stephen R. Covey and A. Roger Merrill. I urge you to examine the book. I find powerful inspiration in its photos and quotations. My favorite is by William Wordsworth: "Come forth into the light of things. Let Nature be your teacher." The book's quotes suggest recognition by many that a certain "leadership character," one steeped in nature and natural laws, exists. I embrace that nature based leadership character.

My own leadership character is a product of my life; nature is, and always has been, a dominant thread of my essential fabric. Embodied within that character are some fundamental truths that I accept without reservation:

- I am a tree, not *the* tree; nor am I the forest.
- A leader serves others, not self.
- It is the ecosystem, not the individual, upon which we collectively depend.

13

- Personal leadership maturation is requisite to becoming a better and more complete leader.
- Always stay alert for nature's lessons and remain willing (and eager) to learn across life's journey.
- Avoid the paradox described by Aldo Leopold in "A Sand County Almanac": "Education, I fear, is learning to see one thing by going blind to another."

For me, the leadership maturation process evolved from leading with my head on an analytical, objective basis to relying more and more upon my heart—a more subjective, empathetic approach. I now know and understand that leading draws strength and wisdom from some pretty basic truths, most of which reside in things natural.

I have matured to recognize that a life well lived requires four levels of fitness. This is the nature of things.

- Physical fitness: taking care of this vessel; avoiding the jaws of the jackal
- Mental fitness: always learning; outfoxing the predator/ competitor; adding a little wood each year
- Emotional fitness: surrounding ourselves with friends and family; the tree as a member of the forest community; contributing to and benefitting from the ecosystem
- Spiritual fitness: believing in something larger than our self; humility and inspiration as constant companions

So, I've discussed my personal basis for adopting the notion of nature based leadership. Where do these reflections lead us? What might we do to help businesses, governmental officials (elected and agency), NGO leaders, citizens, and others better comprehend our individual and collective place in nature, and the lessons for living, learning, and leading expressed in nature? How can we refine the concept of nature based leadership (NBL), develop curricula, and provide educational programs and venues for learning, exchange, and exploration?

I suggest we create a Center for Nature Based Leadership (CNBL), providing a nexus for scholarship, practice, learning, demonstration, and inspiration. Based at Antioch University New England, the center will establish a virtual faculty (scholars affiliated by distance) and Practice Advisory Board (leaders already embracing and practicing the tenets of Natural Leadership).

The CNBL will develop reciprocal partnerships with other entities addressing allied interests. For example, the Biomimicry Institute focuses on an emerging arena that includes borrowing from nature to adopt (mimic) lessons for designing, implementing, managing, and leading. The Antioch University (the broader five-campus system in which AUNE resides) Leadership and Change PhD program is another strong (and, in effect, internal) ally. Conservation Psychology is a rapidly emerging field that encompasses related concepts, principles, and science allied to NBL. Antioch New England stands at the epicenter of Conservation Psychology. One of the field's founders, on the faculty at AUNE, is co-leading with an AUNE colleague, the planned Fall 2015 launch of the nation's first graduate certificate in Conservation Psychology. We'll follow in 2016 with the first graduate degree in the field. We are involving conservation psychology scholars elsewhere as a virtual faculty.

We can (and we must) learn from nature before it is too late. We have just one chance to steward this finite earth. I've offered these thoughts as though we humans, and our society, are somehow removed from nature. Such is not the case. We are integral to nature. Nature sustains us. We, as a species, are powerfully influencing nature itself. In fact, through our collective actions, we are proceeding along a dangerous path toward jeopardizing our future. The Center for Nature Based Leadership can focus learning, stimulate thinking, and inspire action. We can learn from nature's ways to improve our lives, enhance our leadership, and, perhaps, save our species from itself.

I close this essay eighteen months later, in early July 2016, having launched AUNE's Nature Based Leadership Institute in the latter half of last year. I stand by the same underlying NBL principles and tenets—though further refined—as presented in January 2015. I remain deeply resolved about the potency of nature's lessons for our lives.

Ironically, I mentioned earlier in this essay that I went to Urbana University thinking it would be my last position before retirement. The same intention accompanied me when I accepted the AUNE presidency. However, the Antioch University Board of Governors announced in late June 2016 that it would be eliminating all five campus presidents, their administrative assistants, and the campus Boards of Trustees, effective immediately, So much for retirement prophesies! I will remain a NBLI Founder even as I seek yet another executive position in higher education.

The winds of change affect all manner of living, learning, serving, and leading. Nothing is stable, certain, immutable, or guaranteed, including my own career. Once more affirmed by this latest turn of events: change in nature is constant. NBL instructs us to be malleable, flexible, resilient, and always prepared to seek alternatives. There may be another NBL essay in these so-close-to-home career plate tectonics. I'm too consumed at the moment by selling a home, relocating, seeking another position, and completing this manuscript to draft yet another essay. But its title is already on my list.

CHAPTER TWO

Testing the NBL
Concept in Finland

I chaired the University of the Arctic Governing Board from 2006-2008. UArctic is a coalition of 110 colleges and universities, from across the eight northern circumpolar nations, enrolling more than 800,000 students. Antioch University New England, where I served as president through June 30, 2016, is now a UArctic member.

We sited our International Polar Year annual meeting at the University of Lapland, Rovaniemi, Finland in March 2007. The university's rector and I enjoyed a strong kinship that has extended to the present. During the prior winter, he invited me to give the ULapland convocation address in September 2014. I happily accepted. Following my remarks, the university requested a copy. Because my talking points with last-minute, marginal notations would not suffice, I converted those rough notes to prose.

Nature has influenced my thinking considerably over the past few years. The theme is prominent today as I contemplate and write about nature based leadership. I now realize that even before the notion of creating a Nature Based Leadership Institute entered my mind, I had already embedded the concept of leadership influenced by nature into my talking points and stump speeches. Audiences, including the one in Finland, seemed to resonate with the theme.

I offer the text of my remarks as a sort of placeholder and benchmark as my nature based leadership thinking began to take form. I view this as a presentation that operated at the periphery of NBL, yet one that infuses fundamental images and constructs that are nature based.

My friend and colleague Dr. Mauri Yla Kotola, the rector (president) of University of Lapland, invited me to deliver the ULapland convocation address the same year they were marking the university's thirty-fifth anniversary. Rovaniemi, the university's home, sits astride the Arctic Circle and is the largest city in Lapland, as well as Finland's northernmost (and largest) region. The audience included many people who had played a role as ULapland founders (e.g., the founding rector and first chair of the board, Rovaniemi's mayor, the newspaper editor-in-chief, elected officials, faculty, staff, and students).

All of the speakers preceding me, and all those who followed, spoke only Finnish, except for a student leader who spoke briefly in English about higher education at a crossroads. A twelve-piece professional chamber orchestra accompanied the procession and played several pieces during the convocation, including the West Side Story Overture, selected for me by my rector friend, and performed immediately prior to Mauri's introduction of me. I understood the language; I found it lilting, lifting, inspiring, and enjoyable. After the orchestra left the floor, the talks began. I soon contented myself with watching people, listening for reactions, and hoping that I would not disappoint the audience when it became my turn to speak.

I bring you greetings from Antioch University New England in New Hampshire, northeastern USA. I want to thank my dear friend and colleague, Rector Mauri Yla Kotola, for inviting me. To all of you, I extend appreciation and offer congratulations—thirty-five years is a noteworthy achievement! What a pleasure, honor, privilege, and thrill to be here. My message is as applicable to you as it would have been to the audience at my own university's fall convocation two weeks ago. Importantly, we are all fellow citizens of this earth. We are fellow travelers in time, in spirit, in purpose.

I will talk about new beginnings—for you, for me. I'll speak to our responsibility to be Earth stewards, to our imperative to serve to our capacity, to our shared focus on the future "winning victories for humanity." And, I will mention our individual and collective life's journey—leading us to where we need to be.

What credentials do I bring to the lectern: who am I, what am I? The answer is that I (like most of you) wear many hats and represent multiple roles. Here is my own list of descriptors, though not exhaustive: university president, forester, scientist, educator, husband, father, grandfather, lifetime steward of nature and natural resources.

Today marks a new beginning for you. Fall Convocation ushers in a new academic term. You are welcoming a new student cohort. You are forging and refining a new set of dreams and aspirations. Much lies ahead during your anniversary year. This also stands as a series of new beginnings for me. First, my wife and I experienced a life-changing incident on May 3, 2012. As we returned from an evening walk across the campus of Urbana University in Ohio, the driver of a sports utility vehicle ran a stop sign and plowed into us. The event served as a very serious wake-up call, opening our eyes to the reality that life is fleeting and fragile; life is precious. As we recovered, my wife and I vowed that we would live this second life in a manner that is more purposeful, passionate, and faith-based. We reflected on the words of Helen Keller, a 20th Century American author, lecturer, and political activist, who at the age of six lost her sight and hearing to a high fever. She observed during her later years, "Life is a daring adventure or nothing at all." As a result of the accident, I now choose a daring adventure. By this I do not mean dangerously daring, but—rather—boldly daring. We have chosen to make a difference in the world.

That daring acceptance led me to seek new employment that would open doors to making a greater difference. Now, I have been at such an institution since July 1, 2013. My presidency at Antioch University

New England is in full alignment with this second life. Antioch's strong sentiment toward service to humanity remains in our DNA more than a century and a half after the institution's founder implored us to give back to the world.

We're an institution that serves only graduate students; we have a thousand enrollments with a two-thirds to one-third ratio of master's to doctoral students. We hold to the university's tag line, "Because the world needs you now." Our adult working students are drawn to us either because they have already reached an inflection point or because they seek to transform their life and career. A new beginning means new dreams and visions.

Each of you has dreams for career, life, service. I urge you to embrace them, cling to them, cherish them, and bring life to them. Napoleon Hill said that dreams and visions are "the children of your soul." I say to you, nourish those children!

I, too, have my dreams and visions. I long to leave this world a better place for having passed through it. I am determined to give full measure to living, and to making a positive difference. I am committed to tapping the power and the passion of my dreams and visions. I hope you are as well.

My university and yours view education as a learning process that distills to three verbs: see, feel, act. "Seeing," means to view beyond superficially, to see multiple dimensions, and to secure understanding and evaluate implications. It implies seeing deeply enough to feel empathy and to generate a desire to address the issue. And it entails translating that desire to action. Effective education is a process that enables us to see, implores us to feel, and inspires us to act.

We can't each save the whole world. Instead, we can each do our own small part. We can't just hope that tomorrow will be brighter; we must act to make it better.

Yanee, the student who spoke prior to me, hit a seminal point. Yes, "all education is at a crossroads." In fact, our life, our society, and our future are all at a crossroads. Our politicians cannot and will not take us to a brighter future. It is, instead, up to us. It is up to you. It's time for your (and our) daring adventure to begin!

We must act with the strength of our convictions and to the level of our fullest capacity, all in service to humanity. We need to act in service to a future that only we can shape; this is not service in the future, but service today for the future. This is service aimed at "winning victories for humanity."

I end with two quotes, the first from mid-twentieth century Pulitzer Prize winning author and playwright, Louis Bromfield. Bromfield bought an old, worn out farm in the US Midwest in 1938. He devoted his life to rehabilitating the land on Malabar Farm, the name he gave to his property, which he left to the State of Ohio. The park brochure includes a 1945 Bromfield quote: "The adventure at Malabar is by no means finished...The land came to us out of eternity and when the youngest of us associated with it dies, it will still be here. The best we can hope to do is to leave the mark of our fleeting existence upon it, to die knowing that we have changed a small corner of the earth for the better by wisdom, knowledge, and hard work." May those words serve as a metaphor for your life and for mine.

I urge you, as you launch this new academic year (and celebrate the university's thirty-fifth anniversary), to be prepared. Be prepared to leave your own mark on some small corner of this world. Dedicate yourself to a higher calling—a greater purpose. Be prepared to make a difference in the lives of others. Begin your own daring adventure.

I'll close with a final quote that applies to my own life, career, and vocation. In "The Long Dark Tea Time of the Soul," Douglas Adams observed, "I may not have gone where I intended to go, but I think I have ended up where I needed to be." May this convocation begin your journey to where you need to be.

A new friend at the University of Tromso in Norway presented to me a book of proverbs by the Sami (Northern Scandinavia's indigenous peoples). The author starts and ends his book with complementary proverbs. The Sami are historically nomadic, following their reindeer herds across the seasons from summer grazing areas to wintering grounds. The opening proverb states, "It is better to be on a journey than to stay at one place." I'm reminded of my own nomadic career track that has taken my wife Judy and me through twelve interstate moves. Our journey has now taken us "home" to Alabama. The final proverb echoes the first: "A flying bird will always find something; a bird that only stays home will find nothing." Had we stayed where we grew up in the central Appalachians, we may have found nothing. Instead, our flight has landed us at places we needed to be, places we did not even know existed.

In the ULapland convocation remarks above, I had not yet framed my message in terms of nature based leadership. Yet elements of NBL wove through those remarks. In fact, NBL has been evolving and crystalizing within me for many years. It is finally named and brought to life now that have I sorted through and tested its dimensions.

CHAPTER THREE

Is Nature Based Leadership Real?

The Impetus for NBL

Human population now stands at approximately seven and a half billion individuals, each one unique among the teeming masses. Collectively as an Earth society we seem lost, wandering aimlessly and ravaging the very nature that sustains us, even as we inflict (and tolerate) emotional, intellectual, and social carnage. Within the context of this environmental, emotional, intellectual, and social milieu, we hunger for a new view, a different perspective for securing a more certain and positive future.

Far too few of our global citizens understand or appreciate that we as a species and society are totally dependent upon this earth that sustains us. Jared Diamond (in "Collapse: How Societies Choose to Fail or Succeed") spoke of the demise of the once magnificent society on Easter Island in the Pacific Ocean. He observed that the metaphor is so obvious. Like Earth itself, Easter Island stands isolated. Diamond elaborated that once the Easter Island civilization suffered environmental degradation nearing calamity, they could neither leave nor expect help from elsewhere. This One Earth is our "Easter Island," our mote of dust in the vast darkness of space. No one from without will come to rescue us from ourselves. Pope Francis implored us, in his 2015 "Encyclical on Caring for Our Common Home," to awaken before we cross a frightening threshold.

We humans are blessed with remarkable capacities and abilities. We express our intelligence via the five portals: mind, heart, body, spirit, and soul. We have the metaphorical senses to look, see, feel, and act. And we must act now, before we topple over the abyss. We will not act unless we feel deeply about the cause and its urgency. We will not feel unless we see the need—deeply and emphatically. We will not see unless we look for the peril that escapes our societal blindness. We need to begin now to systematically remove the blinders, open our eyes, inspire vision, generate deep feelings, and motivate action.

The Antioch University New England way unlocks the portals through a science-based, experiential learning journey that enables, inspires, and compels students to look, see, feel, and act. The Nature Based Leadership Institute that resides there seeks to open the portals for individuals, companies, agencies, governments, NGOs, or any entity intent upon more effectively living, learning, serving, and leading.

What is Nature Based Leadership?

A team of fifteen NBL founders who are scholars and practitioners from across the country continues to struggle to reach a consensus definition. Some founders lean toward a scholarly construct. I want to employ the concepts in an accessible way, so that it will pass my "Dr. Dirt Test." This is the email moniker that my dear soil scientist, fellow forester friend, and decades-long colleague Dr. John Stanturf employs. I've shared some of my NBL thinking with John over the past few months. His response has consistently been, "Steve, I hear you. Yet, I do not see how NBL differs from more traditional leadership thinking that applies ethics and Earth stewardship-guided principles and tenets." He and I recently agreed to another Skype call to explore. We also concurred that real progress may await in-person conversation inspired by an adult beverage or two. So my objective is to define NBL in a way that passes Dr. Dirt's scrutiny, not an easy task. John is a tough guy who does not cotton to academic hyperbole. We have since met by Skype and Dr. Dirt is beginning to see the NBL light. We will explore more deeply when we meet over a bottle of good single malt scotch.

My Role in NBLI

Upon departing NC State in 2004 for a new gig as the chancellor at University of Alaska Fairbanks, my colleagues presented to me a copy of "The Nature of Leadership," a coffee table book of Dewitt Jones' nature photos accompanied by inspiring quotes. I keep it handy for the many presentations I make, borrowing shamelessly from its pages. My NC State friends gave me that book because of my love of nature and our work together to create the Shelton Leadership Development Center. Several of us had also secured Kellogg Foundation funding to establish a Food Systems Leadership Institute at NC State. I am a student of leadership, an advocate for responsible Earth stewardship, and a champion for making the world a better place. What more fitting university to establish the NBL Institute than at an institution like AUNE, where the fervor is strong, and the heritage is deep.

However, I am not a leadership *scholar*. I don't publish refereed articles in academic leadership journals. I am a practitioner rather than a theorist. For goodness sakes, I am a forester who has long subscribed to the notion that knowledge adds value only when it is applied. How do we define (in a way that clears the Dr. Dirt Test), and then apply, nature based leadership? Over the years, I have come to accept that I am more the NBL poet, steeped deeply in appreciating the wonder, magic, awe, beauty, and inspiration in nature, and seeing the imperative to apply such "softer" elements to living, learning, serving, and leading. I've watched people and enterprises fail miserably when they focus entirely on cold, heartless, numbing facts, figures, and empirical metrics at the expense of the human dimension. So I insist upon heart, passion, and inspiration in my own leadership.

I recall reminding colleagues over the years, "People don't care how much you know until they know how much you care." I have come to care deeply about NBL and the ways through which we perceive: mind, heart, body, soul, and spirit. My own leadership construct has transitioned from primarily objective and empirical, to subjective and empathic. Balance sheets and profit and loss statements are still paramount, yet the root of performance taps into a substrate of enabling, motivating, and inspiring individuals as well as the team.

The example I offered early in this book about climbing Quigley and suddenly seeing Mt. McKinley rising up thousands of white, vertical feet above me is an example, a firsthand metaphor, for learning, living, serving, and leading. It is still interesting to me that I experienced that awesome sight during my first university CEO role. I consider it my number one lesson for NBL: the essential role of humility and inspiration.

I am NBLI's humility and inspiration conscience. My fellow founders can swim in the academic and scholarly end of the pool. I will play in the heart and soul end, insisting and cajoling all to bear ever in mind that NBL adds nothing to the art and practice of leadership unless we infuse the wonder of nature and her lessons learned over eons of evolutionary discipline.

Employ Conservation

A Guest Essay by Ron Dodson

Being a child in a small mid-western Indiana town, my earliest and fondest memories are of spending time on the farm of my grandparents. The sights and sounds of the farm and the way that nature was weaved into every day decisions forged the foundation of my life. As an adult, I was trained as a wildlife biologist; by profession I have been an educator. As a schoolteacher, an executive of one conservation organization or another, an author and consultant, I have spent the better part of thirty-five years working to encourage people to become more aware of and connected with nature and natural resource management.

While living in Kentucky, one educational project that I am very proud of was serving as a regional director of the Alaska Coalition in 1979-80. This effort included work in Washington, D.C., educating elected officials from the lower forty-eight states about the importance of Alaska. A year's worth of educating culminated in President Carter signing the Alaska Lands Act, which doubled the size of the national park system. I am proud to have been in the White House on the day that President Carter signed the act into law.

In 1987 I reincorporated and re-founded the Audubon Society of New York State, Inc. (ASNYS), which is the second oldest Audubon Society in the United States. In an effort to motivate people from all walks of life to become engaged in conservation management, I created the Audubon Cooperative Sanctuary System (including programs for schools, farms, backyards, corporate properties, golf courses and municipalities) and the Audubon Signature Cooperative Sanctuary Program, which was established to work with people who are in the planning and design stages of development. Today, people are involved in these programs across the United States as well as in twenty-six other countries around the globe.

To expand the focus beyond single properties, I created the Sustainability Campaign of the International Sustainability

Council-Audubon (ISC-Audubon) where I presently volunteer as chairman. In that regard, I am working with government agencies, universities, businesses, and not-for-profit organizations to advocate and assist in the development of sustainable living and lifestyle practices.

From feeding the chickens, milking the cows, tending the garden, and observing the nature of my grandparent's farm, I have planned and designed nearly two hundred wildlife sanctuaries around the world, created numerous education programs aimed at getting people more aware of and involved with nature and natural resource management, and I have worked with thousands of people in regard to wildlife and habitat conservation.

My personal and professional life has revolved around nature. Still, we continue to witness the loss of more and more habitat and the loss of more and more species of wildlife. We are in the midst of a great extinction and that is why it is critically important that each and every one of us do what we can to employ conservation landscape management practices where we live, work, and play.

Bio

Ron Dodson is an award winning conservationist and author who has traveled the world, and written several books about nature and natural resource management. He has served as Regional Vice-President of the National Audubon Society, he re-founded of the Audubon Society of New York State and now serves as Chair of the International Sustainability Council-Audubon (ISC-Audubon). Dodson created several award winning education programs that are presently being employed around the globe, and he enjoys writing about interesting places where nature can be enjoyed, while at the same time providing information that can help conserve natural resources and the environment.

CHAPTER FOUR

Who Cares About Nature Based Leadership?

Just this year during a period of impassioned writing, I visited Mom in northern West Virginia. I had placed in a nice folder double-sided print outs of eight of my emerging NBL essays, and I delivered them to her. These were powerfully personal, reflecting on experiences and reminiscences from my early years. Some generated tears as I remembered, contemplated, synthesized, and typed at the keyboard. I thought, "Won't she be impressed, and emotionally moved." After all, her son (though he's sixty-four, a little old to be showing his homework to his ninety-one-year-old mom) wrote these words from the depth of his soul and heart. I imagined her reading and rereading, moved herself to tears, and thinking, "Wow, this is great writing; I can't believe this is my son!"

I called two weeks later, eager to hear her reaction. She said quite unemotionally, "I only found two mistakes," and she proceeded to tell me where I had erred: in noting her age, and the date of Dad's death. Mom said nothing about quality, her impressions or emotional reaction, or any other evocations from the raw heart, soul, and spirit I had poured into those forty pages. So how is this story of my own mother's reaction (or lack thereof) to my writing related to nature based leadership? This is a good question that I've struggled to understand and address.

Here's where I've landed in my thinking. While Mom and Dad both shaped and sculpted the boy and young man who exited their home forty-five years ago, it was Dad who ignited my nature based passions and lifelong love affair with the outdoors. Dad would have read the essays, felt their emotion, and shed tears. It was Mom who led me to reading and ultimately, I suppose, to writing. She remains an avid reader, yet her preferred genre has never evidenced even a thread of nature, especially nonfiction. She has never read "A Sand County Almanac," my secular Bible of conservation, ecology, and land ethics. I believe that Mom would not appreciate Aldo Leopold's ultimate statement of conservation: "A thing is right when it tends to preserve the integrity, stability and beauty of the biotic community. It is wrong when it tends otherwise."

Nor would she receive Leopold's observation about preserving wildness: "All conservation of wildness is self-defeating, for to cherish we must see and fondle, and when enough have seen and fondled, there is no wilderness left to cherish." My mom would not know the name John McPhee, who in my mind stands at the pinnacle of translating the magic and wonder of nature and natural forces for lay readers. She would not feel the power and might of McPhee's single statement summation of our dynamic planet in Basin and Range: "If by some fiat I had to restrict all this writing to one sentence, this is the one I would choose: The summit of Mt. Everest is marine limestone."

Mom is not dull; she retains her mental agility. Simply, her interests lie elsewhere, directed to other arenas. My writing did not reach her. I should not have been surprised. I regret feeling disappointment. I will gather the folder when I next visit—after I give her a big hug, and thank her for launching me into a topical and professional world that is mostly foreign to her.

My formative years ushered me into an education that has changed my life. Mom influenced my ambition, stirred my passion, and spirited me to gain invaluable knowledge in my chosen discipline. I suppose, at the very least, she inspired a latent desire to translate my own deep feelings into persuading others to look, see, feel, and act. I seek to stimulate others, to plant the seeds of reasoned insight, profound understanding, and absolute appreciation for the wonder of nature and our absolute dependence upon it.

Mom's done her part. She does not now need to further stroke, persuade, and enable her considerably adult son in the pursuit he has chosen. That's his business, his choice, his passion. I don't mean to be so cavalier. I certainly don't want to diminish Mom, to suggest that she is anything but an early-life potent force, influencing where I now stand in confirming and cementing my life's work. We've moved past each other in this arena. She's okay with me, but she is not interested in playing a role where she has no direct interest.

I've moved beyond my own disappointment. Now, my concern is whether or not these writings will attract anybody's attention. I hope so. I'm really enjoying drafting my way through these essays. Writing has opened my inner view, helped me understand my own philosophy and Earth ethic as I translate my thoughts and reflections to text. It may sound silly, but contemplating doesn't require much thought. Thinking can be shallow, a simple flow of feelings and impressions. Snippets of ideas, images, and rough conclusions. Writing, on the other hand, demands deep thinking, probing questions, and logical constructions. Via writing I'm learning a great deal about myself, and I'm seeing ever more clearly into the concept, philosophy, and potential practice of nature based leadership.

My challenge, shared by my fellow Nature Based Leadership Institute founders, is how we identify and reach those for whom my words might stir resonance, appreciation, and response. Certainly, we among the fifteen NBLI founders will read, resonate, and find inspiration in at least a few of the selected essays. Are there fifteen other potential readers who might? One hundred fifty, one thousand, many thousands? I want to spread the gospel, to ignite a movement. I want to bring sight to those who are blind to recognizing that we are a society and a species at peril. I want to awaken leaders and potential leaders to nature's wisdom, and to her simple lessons for living, for learning, for serving and leading.

Here in this seeming endless presidential election season, I recall the political adage that a campaign need not focus on voters who already have committed to our candidate. Nor need we focus on those ensconced deeply in the opponent's camp. Instead, the campaign should target those who might be influenced to our side. Such is not quite so simple in my crusade to spark a nature based leadership movement. I see three camps:

- Those who already embrace an Earth stewardship ethic—they may or may not comprehend the precepts of NBL. They likely have not experienced the explicit and implicit lessons for leadership written in or inspired by nature. We must focus on them even as we reach out to enfold those in the second category.
- Those who might be persuaded—our hope with this second group is to accomplish two ends. First, we want them to embrace an Earth ethic in their lives. And second, as with the first category, we want to see them understand and adopt our NBL lessons.
- My Mother—I know when I'm wasting my time.

So who cares about nature based leadership? We all should. We should all adopt a personal Earth ethic. Pope Francis agrees. His 2015 Encyclical does not employ the term "Earth ethic." Yet that, along with its environmental, social, and economic justice theme, is what he implores. Pope Francis suggests that the nearly one and half billion Catholics should care about the set of ideas that constitute nature based leadership. The Encyclical's audience is not limited to a Catholic readership. Pope Francis views its precepts as essential to the entire family of Man. Our Earth and society and its future are in unprecedented peril, he argues.

I contend that nature based leadership is not the answer. Instead,

NBL is <u>an</u> answer. NBL is one avenue for addressing the problem. On closer examination, NBL may not even be an answer. Rather, NBL may be one path to lead us to answers. NBL is a vehicle for directing us to acknowledge our peril, and to consciously integrate that awareness into every decision we make. NBL is a direction, a way of shaping and then bringing an Earth ethic into our daily lives, one that is both personal and professional. On final reflection, NBL may be an effective vehicle for leading us to questions without which we will not seek answers.

NBL is learning and borrowing from nature in a manner that opens our minds to contemplating an Earth ethic imperative. NBL reminds us, both subtly and emphatically, that we are integral to nature, not apart from it. Ironically, Mom knows she lives in nature. Her home sits on a hilltop in the central Appalachians. It looks west across rolling hills to the Allegany Front, the eastern continental divide, where the tortured, folded strata of the ridge and valley meet the nearly horizontal formations of the plateau, and the highlands beyond. My mother hears and feels the wind buffeting her roof and walls. She embraces the warm sun as she sits in her living room by the south-facing window. She watches the snow coat her fields, and then celebrates its melting. She watches deer and turkey from her window. She observes and appreciates the changing seasons. We talk about the weather when I call.

That's a start; Mom is not blind to nature as so many are. She simply does not feel the beat of nature based leadership, to which my own life dances, ebbs, and flows. Yet she does sense, appreciate, and understand how nature affects her life. She is far from hopeless. She would not speak about an environmental ethic, yet I believe in her own way she understands our obligation to steward this Earth. Mom does not care about NBL, yet she does care about our relationship to this Earth.

I'm feeling less and less disappointed by Mom's reaction to my essays. I may do more than simply collect that set of eight when I next visit. I may actually explore the topic with her. The worst she can do is dispassionately remind me of my two errors. Perhaps I will learn something of great value when we talk. Maybe she can help me understand more clearly the topic of this essay. Perhaps there is a portal even to Mom.

And, perhaps there is a way to reach beyond the NBLI Founders. Where and how do we begin? I believe this book of essays is a start. We plan to offer NBL workshops and short courses. We will speak at professional meetings on leadership. We will recruit new missionaries, ambassadors to the cause. We've already created the NBL Institute. We're generating interest among faculty and students at Antioch University New England, and beyond. Our founders are carrying the message far and wide. We anticipate launching a formal NBL for-credit certificate within the year. We see a master's NBL concentration within eighteen months. We're planting the seed with foundations, NGOs, and agencies. We are seeking corporate and business interests.

So who does care about nature based leadership? We will answer that question. We hope to be overwhelmed by the level of interest we generate. Our goal is to plant the seeds, nurture the germinants, cultivate the seedlings, and eventually share the yield. I place a favorite quote from Robert Louis Stevenson beneath the signature line of every email I send. It seems a good way to close this essay. "Don't judge each day by the harvest you reap but by the seeds that you plant."

CHAPTER FIVE

Little Green Heron

My list of lifetime regrets stands at forty-nine. I don't mean I regret every "I should not have said, did, acted, or behaved the way I did." Instead, these are the ones of significance that have traveled with me, some for four decades and more. These are regrets about hurting somebody or something; they are not those that simply made me look dumb, or feel stupid. I started the list about twenty years ago. I lost it once and rewrote it. When I found the one I had lost, the new one matched perfectly. These regrets are deeply etched, but so are their lessons. Not to worry, I am not about to recite all four dozen. But I do want to share just one of the regrets and the corresponding lessons relevant to my thinking about nature based leadership.

I grew up in Cumberland, Maryland at the western terminus of the Chesapeake and Ohio Canal, constructed in the mid-nineteenth century; its eastern terminus is in Georgetown near Washington D.C. Ours was an outdoor family. Dad maintained an entire menu of fishing holes within an hour or so of home. Battie Mixon, a restored and re-watered section of the canal just eighteen miles away, offered sunfish, bass, catfish, and a few other species. We fished there at least half a dozen times every summer. Dad would fish and allow me the freedom to wander the shoreline as long as I stayed in sight. Once I reached adolescence, he no longer insisted I stay within view.

On one such trip, I was perhaps twelve or thirteen and the fish weren't biting enough to command my full attention. Just to the right (south) of the towpath, a linear depression also held water, but it was shallower than the fishing hole and was being reclaimed by sediment and emerging vegetation. (The depression was the area from which canal construction engineers took additional fill for the elevated towpath as well as the next lock half a mile from the access road.)

I often watched that wetland for turtles, snakes, birds, dragonflies, and other critters. That particular occasion I saw a wading bird that I can now identify (remembering the image I'd seen that day) as a little green heron; though I did not know the bird's identity at the time. What I did understand is that at more than a hundred feet from me, the bird offered a tempting rock target for an early adolescent boy. I found the perfect rock and, without considering the consequences, aimed and threw it at the impossibly small target. I hit the beautiful little green heron in the head; the bird toppled. I waited for it to regain its footing, or to rise and fly off. It did neither. I did not celebrate my accuracy nor congratulate my "lucky" throw. I stood stunned, suffering silently for the foolish act I had just perpetrated. I can close my eyes today, fifty years later, and still picture the image clearly and in vivid detail. And in that moment of remembering, I feel the regret as though I had just this moment slung the rock.

I did not tell Dad; in fact I told no one until writing this essay. I've killed birds since then, upland game birds as a licensed hunter: woodcock, pheasant, ruffed grouse, quail, and turkey. But no more errant rocks. Such birds as the little green heron are protected by law, and now safe by virtue of my own awareness of unintended consequences. My guilt and shame live on, fueling a palpable regret, unabated by time.

The shallow, warm-water slough surface was green in spots with filamentous algae that day; I still see the bird's floating, delicate corpse as I walked closer, hoping against hope that my missile had done less than mortal harm. Not so. I suppose my lament relates more to the symbol of the bird than of the actual death. I ended the life of a creature that brought magic to an otherwise dismal setting. Though it was not a dismal place to me, few people see the beauty and wonder in the stagnant, algae-coated warm water in which that heron fished. I found delight and wonder in the place even then: the sunning turtles aligned on fallen logs, the witch doctors (dragonflies) darting just above the green surface, the muskrat tracing a 'V' through the still water. The little green heron had stood there fixed, and transfixed, watching for edible life, waiting patiently, fearing nothing.

My projectile came without warning. Evolution had not alerted his nerves, sensors, and reflexes to adolescent-heaved stones. I robbed a vibrant ecosystem of a precious participant for no purpose other than to test my arm. Maybe I am further saddened because that selfish act of violence and waste symbolizes my own species' careless disregard for so much that is nature and natural. We tend too often to ask of other life, "Does it add material value?" If not, then go ahead: toss a rock in its direction. So much of what we do is blind to the intrinsic values that economics ignore. Isn't it time we gain awareness, learn to attribute real value, and stop throwing rocks to test an arm? I remember Leopold's wisdom once again. He spoke of the complexities and interconnectedness of our natural systems. He asked in "Round River: The Journals of Aldo Leopold": "Who but a fool would discard seemingly useless parts? To keep every cog and wheel is the first precaution of intelligent tinkering." I ache for that individual little green heron, and I always will. I paid the deep price of guilt, humility, and shame to learn and accept a life-lasting lesson. Every action yields consequences. Nothing should be done for which consequences are not apparent. Every cog adds value, some beyond measure, some timeless. If only everyone practiced the art of intelligent tinkering!

I also now know that a conscience doesn't develop from reading a manual. I learned that late summer afternoon the power of recognized guilt and responsibility as soon as the heron fell. I've held myself accountable for fifty years. A cog in the wheel of life is connected to the whole. No little green heron stands alone, separate from all else. How can our Nature Based Leadership Institute open many more eyes to such lessons of interconnectivity, responsibility, and consequences? How can we discourage rock-slinging in all its metaphorical dimensions? How can we illuminate the consequences of every decision? Perhaps most importantly, how do we instill an Earth Ethic (a disciplined self-awareness and conscience) in every business, NGO, organization, and individual? How do we successfully encourage, develop, and instill an obligation to be responsible Earth stewards?

Perhaps most importantly, how do we apply nature's lessons to all aspects of our lives as we learn, offer, and lead? That afternoon so many years ago, I looked at the little green heron. But I looked blindly. I did not see the life and its place in the wetlands ecosystem, nor the wetlands and its place on the landscape. I saw only a target to serve me in a brief moment of self-absorption and shameful entertainment—a sort of contest to test my arm. Only after I exacted from the bird the toll of death, did I both see and feel. I saw the act for what it was, and I felt the consequence and harm from my foolish throw. I could not undo the deed. Instead, I decided to learn from that day, and to apply the lesson time and time again.

Now, I am embedding the lesson in the fabric of our Nature Based Leadership Institute, and sharing this tale for the benefit of those engaged, and for the many we hope to touch. All lessons distill to stories. I will take the little green heron to the end of my life's journey, telling and retelling my story and the fateful role he played.

CHAPTER SIX

Jack Berglund's Belief in Me

I put the following words in the acknowledgements section of my May 1987 doctoral dissertation: "I dedicate this document to the memory of Dr. John V. Berglund, who was the guiding force in my pursuit of the degree, and who served as my major professor until his death in November, 1986. I came to ESF because Jack was here. I was fortunate to have studied and worked under his direction. Through that association, I benefitted both professionally and personally. He was an outstanding mentor and a good friend."

Dr. Berglund was nineteen years younger than I am now when I unsuccessfully administered CPR in the parking lot at Hunters Lodge Restaurant near Salamanca, NY in November 1986. Jack was one of five natural resources professionals who shaped, inspired, and changed me forever. We never spoke of what I now call nature based leadership. I have grasped and given presence and a name to the concept only over the past couple of years. Yet I know he would have embraced the notion. We spent enough time together that I am sure Jack would agree that our life and professional lessons are, through and through, the workings of nature.

First (and Lasting) Impressions

I met my mentor the summer of my sophomore year, 1971. A Greyhound bus dropped me in Warrensburg, NY for the eight-week forestry field experience at the nearby State University of New York College of Environmental Science and Forestry (ESF) Pack Forest field station. Warrensburg is near Lake George, still a garish tourist destination (I admit my nature based prejudice) that is everything the forever-wild Adirondacks are not. I can't recall how I made it from the bus station to Pack. As a forestry transfer from Allegany Community College in Cumberland, MD, all of this was new to me: New York; the Adirondacks; SUNY ESF; Pack Forest; the sixty other forestry students, many who already knew each other from their first two years at ESF.

Jack would have been at home in the logging woods. In fact, a native of northwestern Pennsylvania (Johnsonburg), he worked his way through college in the woods, providing pulpwood to the mill in his hometown. He looked the part. Bull of the woods. Built like a linebacker. Strong hands, square jaw. Field shirts with sleeves rolled.

I recall only three professors from Pack that summer. Richard Lea, Pack Forest Camp Director; we called him "The General." Always hurrying, concerned with the details, the logistics. In retrospect, I marvel at the burden of feeding, corralling, and housing sixty students. No wonder he seemed frenetic. Dr. William "Bill" Johnson, a slender Virginian who had recently come to ESF from a forest products company in the southeast. Bill merits his own story for another essay. Bill emerged as a mentor, hero, and coach for me. He's one of my five. He assisted me in landing my first professional forestry position back with the company (Union Camp Corporation) he had served. And Dr. John "Jack" Berglund. Jack was thirty-one years old, not long beyond earning his PhD at ESF. He seemed seasoned and wise; thirty-one could have been fifty. He was the consummate forester I aspired to be. He knew the woods and his craft. His specialty was silvics, the ecology of tree species in forests. His knowledge was deep and flawless. Jack exuded confidence. I revered him. He was what this young, shy, Appalachian introvert could never be.

He appreciated during that summer—and during the subsequent two years in Syracuse, ESF's campus home—that I was a ready student, an achiever, with a good woods sense of my own. He commended me for gaining three summers of field experience with the Maryland Forest Service, and for finding a work-study position on the ESF campus in the forest entomology lab. He must have seen some of his own work ethic and blue-collar stock in me. He and Bill Johnson were dear friends and superlative colleagues. They laughed and worked together at a level of friendship and camaraderie that is absent in my own work today. They were professionally inseparable. And they apparently were convinced that I embodied something they wanted to nurture. I see this now in the forty-plus years rear view mirror. I only knew back then that I wanted to perform for them, to please them.

That wasn't hard to do. I simply loved the subject matter they taught, and they were the best. Jack's silvics and Bill's silviculture set me afire. I wanted to know everything, and they were there ready and eager to make sure I could, and did. Allow me to stick to Jack, and fight the temptation to include Bill in every aspect of this essay.

Hatching a Hidden Career Plan for Steve

Yet, I want to keep them together for just another few paragraphs. These gentlemen conspired in a way I have just recently deciphered. Jack and Bill knew that I wanted to work in forestry. They understood my first-generation-to-college, blue collar upbringing. They knew I married between junior and senior year. They knew that professional forestry experience would serve me well at this stage of life and career. They felt that while I could have tracked seamlessly into successive graduate degrees, that I needed boots-on-the-ground experience. That's what they, too, would have done had they been given a second chance. They committed and conspired, I am now certain, to help plot my professional trajectory, to keep me within their reach and eventually attract me back for an advanced degree. Bill shortly thereafter accepted a forestry position at NC State University. He died within a couple of years at age forty-six, collapsing and succumbing during a ten-kilometer road race. The mantle fell to Jack to monitor and eventually cajole me to tackle the advanced degree. Only the act of writing this has brought me to understand and appreciate their conspiracy. I am grateful to the point of tears as I type. I loved these men in a way I can only now really grasp.

I am eternally grateful that they did not, as so many professors do, encourage (persuade, coerce, and badger) me to immediately enter a master's program. I recall one of my undergraduate professors urging me toward graduate school. He said, "A student of your merit would be foolish to simply take a job." I responded, "A student of my accomplishment and potential would be foolish not to first secure professional experience." Jack and Bill launched me into the security and wisdom to enter my profession as a practitioner, not as a scholar or student. And that has made all the difference!

I don't remember how I said goodbye to Jack at that launching. The introvert probably simply shook a hand and felt too self-conscious to express any true or deep feelings. It's only as I pass through my seventh decade that I can say what needs to be said. Jack and I stayed in touch. I joined the Society of American Foresters (SAF) and occasionally saw Jack at gatherings. He never failed to inquire with great interest in my life, both professional and personal. He watched my career at Union Camp with genuine interest. As those twelve years passed, he gradually ramped his encouragement for me to think about a PhD. He recognized that the significant experience I had gained in four years leading the company's tree nutrition and forest fertilization research project had accomplished the equivalent of a master's degree. My final three years with Union Camp found me managing a unit responsible for five hundred square miles of company owner forestland. Jack pushed harder, persuading me to think more deeply about my own professional future and the life pressures bearing on me, pressures of timing that meant it might be now or never for that PhD brass ring. He prevailed.

The Plan's Next Step

I was Alabama Woodlands Land Manager, a mid-level management position in a Fortune 500 paper and allied products manufacturing corporation. Another step would lift me from my professional natural resources passion. Our kids were seven and five. We were approaching our mid-thirties. Either we do the doctoral degree immediately, when there was still time for a redirected career following the degree, or forget about it. Jack struck a hard bargain. He said that if I kept my end of the bargain (to dedicate myself completely to my doctoral studies), he would make sure I finished in three years. By this time, Jack was terminally ill. He might make it through my doctoral program; he might not. He wanted this as much as I did. Judy and I decided that we believed in him enough to turn our world upside down and inside out. I committed, and I have never looked back. He changed my life. I took a leap of faith and it changed my life.

I started my doctoral work with an eight-year-old son and a six-year-old daughter in a downsized home with my wife, to whom I had been married for thirteen years. I no longer had a comfortable salary with annual bonus eligibility or the company car. Instead, I used a second hand vehicle to make it back and forth to campus. We knew we would live less comfortably for those three years. Yet Jack arranged a fellowship with a tuition waiver accompanied by a significant graduate stipend, easing the pace of dipping into savings. Stepping aside from a position with sixty employees and a greater than six million dollar annual operating budget, I found myself back in classes. What an adjustment!

Jack showed pure enthusiasm about having me on campus. He genuinely valued the practical experience I brought with me. He asked me to lead a newly created ESF-led inter-industry cooperative, the

Northeast Petroleum—Forest Resources Cooperative (NEP-FRC). It seemed as if the Pennsylvania crude oil deposits in NW Pennsylvania and SW New York were once again economically viable to produce. Most subsurface mineral rights were held separately from surface ownership. Surface rights included the coincidentally highly valuable Allegheny hardwood forests of cherry, ash, maple, and oak. The owners were at odds and conflicts were reaching fever pitch, hence the need for an education, demonstration, and discussion forum led by an objective, natural resources-based university steeped in applicable science and historic issue resolution. Jack named me the founding executive director, thus the respectable stipend and tuition waiver for services rendered. Jack and I traveled frequently to the NEP-FRC region, often meeting at either the US Forest Service Allegheny Forestry Lab at Warren, PA or at the Allegany State Park headquarters near Salamanca, NY.

A Funded Dissertation Project

Hammermill Paper Company owned thousands of acres of the region's valuable hardwood forests in support of its Erie, PA mill. Seeking to ease the inter-industry tension and conflict, Hammermill helped create NEP-FRC as a charter member. Jack respected Hammermill's Woodlands Division VP Richard "Dick" Wallace. Dick recognized Jack's woods savvy and relied upon his sound judgment and deep understanding of forestry. Together they proposed a dissertation focus for me, complete with Hammermill providing full project funding.

I could not have been more excited about the nature and scope of the research problem: evaluating the soil-site relationship for Allegheny hardwoods right there in the NEP-FRC region. Jack had performed a complementary analysis for his Penn State master's research. I celebrated the level of funding, which covered the full budget for the fieldwork as well as subsequent lab analyses and analytics. I had agonized over what to tackle, how to fund it, and when to begin. Jack had brought the PhD into focus. A full-fledged field-based project in a forest I loved, meeting the real needs of a vibrant forest products company, and modeled in the spirit of Jack's professional passion. The project and its support enabled us to develop a detailed timetable, placing within reach the three-year agreement that Jack and I had.

We mapped a plan for all that lay ahead. I had completed my doctoral coursework by then, or so Jack made abundantly clear. I wanted to take several more courses which offered great appeal. Jack said "no," unequivocally and non-negotiably. He said simply, "We have an agreement." Together, we planned a date certain for me completing the degree—December 1987.

Jack began to sense another end. He had begun to more noticeably fade. He looked older, frailer. When we visited my field sites we mostly drove and talked, perhaps finding one or two sampling plots within an easy stroll. He labored with even the slightest exertion. He arranged for Dr. Edwin White, already on my PhD Committee, to chair the concluding days, weeks, or months should Jack not make it to the effort's conclusion.

Jack's End

We were heading to the Park for yet another NEP-FRC Board meeting. We arrived in the area at dinnertime. We headed toward the Hunter's Lodge Restaurant on that wet evening, already dark in mid-November. Bob Koepperer, ESF Director of Conferences, had accompanied us. I drove; Jack sat in the front passenger seat. We parked and exited the vehicle. Jack struggled to stand, holding tight to the door. I watched him collapse to the gravel lot as I hurried to that side of the car. Bob and I got him flat on his back. He showed no response. I urged Bob to run inside to seek medical assistance.

I checked for breathing and pulse, then opened his airway and began CPR. I had kept my first aid certification current during my Union Camp years. I went through the motions almost mechanically, not thinking beyond the moment. The EMTs arrived probably within ten to fifteen minutes; I had no sense of time. I recall people filing from the restaurant, standing at the perimeter, watching. Someone offered a handkerchief to avoid the actual mouth-to-mouth. I don't know whether I used it or not; I had already been performing the direct resuscitation for some minutes without it. The EMTs relieved me upon their arrival. They commented almost immediately that he would not make it.

I remember little else beyond absolute numbness. I had Jack's effects in the car. I could not emotionally make the call to his wife Nan. Instead I called Dr. Harry Burry, Director of Forestry Adult and Continuing Education, a colleague of mine and a friend and neighbor of Jack's. Harry hurried to Nan to advise her in person. I remember calling Judy, and little else. Bob and I spent the night in Salamanca, heading back to Syracuse the next morning. To this day, I can see Jack collapsing as though it just happened. I knew when I saw his eyes as he collapsed that my CPR would have little chance of success, yet I gave it all I had. I lost a friend that night, yet in large measure I had come to him two years prior knowing that I would likely lose him.

Return on Jack's Investment in Me

What did I give Jack? I gave him the gift of placing my professional future in his hands at a time when few others would have come to work with a terminally ill professor. I helped him realize a dream that he (and Bill Johnson) had hatched back in 1973. I hope I gave him one more element of purpose while the illness consumed him. I pray that he knew in his final days that I would secure the PhD and then do good work with it.

Thirty years after his death I think of him often. I will never match the indelible image of Jack—the master woodsman, indefatigable, rugged, and confident, the scholar who commanded a room. Yet many times I have tapped his strength (a reservoir deep within me) when I've faced difficulties, or even before taking the microphone as I stand at a lectern. I do not wear the strength as Jack did. I'd have to fake it; Jack feigned nothing. That is how I know he believed in me. He devoted much of his final two years to me. With each year that passes, especially now that I begin to think about my own impending retirement, I am ever more humbled by his selfless commitment to me. How can I repay that steely devotion?

One of my life's regrets is that I did not have the strength (courage) to attend Jack's viewing or his memorial service. I could not bring myself to express my sympathy (and my loss) to Nan or Jack's two children, Joel and Beth. I still feel deep guilt that the young man I was, who accompanied Jack on that final day, could not face the close family he left behind. That lesson was learned and has been applied many times since: never miss an opportunity (or shirk an obligation) to express a deep and kind word or emotion. Never fail to offer real words of comfort and consolation. Shed a tear (or tears) freely and without embarrassment. Emotion (the virtuous kind) should never be wasted.

Nature Based Leadership

How do I bring this essay back to nature based leadership? Everything about Jack was nature based. He saw the same in me. We talked often about the Union Camp career track that would have led me further from my natural resources passion. He wanted me to stay in the nature based professional stream. Not so much for me, but for the good I might do with the advanced degree. He never used these words yet I sincerely believe that he somehow saw his own future in me. He believed that I could be an Earth steward worthy of his investment of precious time and energy, even as his days waned. Writing this essay has been an act of discovery. Jack inspired me to conceive of this notion of nature based leadership, something I did not realize until this very moment.

Nature based leadership demands a deep sense of humility and inspiration. I feel intense humility when I reflect on Jack's devotion to and investment in me. This larger-than-life man saw something in me that I am only now beginning to discover and appreciate. My entire life and career have led toward defining and accepting a fundamental truth: the future of our species depends upon a more palpable, deliberate, and systematic acceptance that all leadership must be nature based. How can it not be if we embrace the simple notion that we are one with nature, not distinct from it? I believe that Jack encouraged me to explore life and career, and then pulled me back for the doctoral degree just before it was too late, because he envisioned a purpose for me. Thirty years after his death I have discovered the purpose: to inspire a new way of thinking about leadership, thinking that can perhaps save us from ourselves.

From this day forward I will more consciously invoke Jack's spirit in my nature based leadership contemplation. What would Jack think, or do? How would he see the Nature Based Leadership Institute emerge and serve? How can I find additional inspiration and motivation knowing that Jack stands with me? How can I employ the greater humility in accepting that, without having a crystal ball more than four decades ago, both Jack Berglund and Bill Johnson, had faith that young forester Steve Jones might actually do something of value in their memory?

Jack now lives within our Nature Based Leadership Institute. He's walking alongside me this morning. I welcome and embrace his support, confidence, and belief. Jack most assuredly would have endorsed the basic premise of nature based leadership—that "all lessons for living, learning, serving, and leading are written indelibly *in* or powerfully inspired *by* nature."

I can recall that wet November night thirty years ago as though it has just happened. I close my eyes, feel the cold dampness, and see Jack collapsing to the puddled gravel surface. I see his empty countenance. My heart aches. But I am buoyed now because I see the smiling, robust bull of the woods striding confidently, holding the NBLI banner high, and saying to a young Bill Johnson, "See, I told you he would amount to something!"

I am wiping tears as my fingers type these final few thoughts.

Inspiration. Humility. Appreciating our place and time in the world. And accepting our obligation to steward this One Earth, our mote of dust in the vast darkness of space. Nothing is more important. How can I return full dividend to Jack's investment? I can do so in the spirit of that long ago dissertation acknowledgement. I mirror it again now: "I dedicate my own nature based leadership journey to the memory of Dr. John V. Berglund, who was the guiding force in my pursuit of a doctoral degree, and who served as my major professor until his death in November, 1986. I came to ESF because Jack was there. I was fortunate to have studied and worked under his direction. Through that association, I benefitted both professionally and personally. He was an outstanding mentor and a good friend. He stands with me now as NBL takes form and strives to make tomorrow attainable and sustainable."

Roots of Leadership

A Guest Essay by John Stanturf

I have always liked trees. I think this intensified to passion at summer camps in the coast redwoods of California, or maybe when our military family was stationed near the Black Forest in southern Germany, or later near the Grunewald in West Berlin. Philosophers have commented on the importance of trees, and scientists today propose that increasing forests is the most immediate way to combat climate change. Yochanan ben Zakkai, a first century rabbi, put the value of trees in practical terms: "If you are planting a tree and you hear that the Messiah has come, finish planting the tree then go and inquire."

Growing up, I never considered that trees would become a career interest; that came later, when I started pursuing higher education at Montana State and Cornell. Eventually, my focus turned to forest soils (or, the dirt that trees grow in). Tree roots are intimately connected to soil at multiple scales: through structural roots that anchor the towering aboveground parts. At smaller and smaller scales, the fine roots and symbiotic mycorrhizal fungi that envelop and invade soil particles seek nutrients and water.

What lessons have I learned from tree roots that have inspired my leadership of groups of scientists and support staff at universities, forest industry, and government research centers? I have learned that root systems, and good leaders, provide support, buffer from disturbances, employ symbiotic relationships, and model entrepreneurial attitudes.

Roots provide physical support by going as deeply as they can, into cracks in bedrock if necessary. These structural roots are the scaffolding on which the other functions hang and perform. A leader must provide a supporting system based on trust and mutual respect that allows the team (or organization) to function smoothly.

But disturbances buffet the forest just as external actors and conditions challenge the team. The nature of the root system determines if a tree will bend or break. The depth of anchored roots and the strength of soil material are determinants. Good—even great—leadership is no guarantee of success, but it can provide a buffer from storms. Success is more than weathering storms; success requires thriving.

Building symbiotic relationships, characterized by win-win situations, is another function of a leader. Just as the symbiosis between the mycorrhizal fungus and the tree root sends nutrients and water to the tree and carbon to the fungus, the leader and the rest of the team must engage in win-win efforts. One of my greatest joys as a leader has been to facilitate and watch individuals on my team excel and be recognized for their achievements. Their thriving nourishes me.

We do not sit back and wait for opportunities (funding, invitations, awards) to come. Entrepreneurship defines my approach to leadership. I encourage and support the rest of the team to seek out nourishment; each looks for opportunities for themselves, for others on the team, or for the whole team. Like roots, they proliferate in the soil.

Bio

John Stanturf is a Senior Scientist with the US Forest Service, Center for Forest Disturbance Science, Athens, GA. His professional experience includes manager of pine silviculture research, Union Camp Corp. and faculty positions at Penn State, University of Pittsburgh, and Cornell University. He received his MSc and PhD in forest soils from Cornell, BSc from Montana State University, and was a Lady Davis Postdoctoral Fellow at the Technion, Israel. The Estonian University of Life Sciences awarded him an honorary doctorate in 2011. Research interests are functional restoration of degraded forests; disturbance and risk in forest management; climate change adaptation; and bioenergy.

CHAPTER SEVEN

Snow in the Arc Light

My elderly mother tells me that her older sister, Geraldine, tried to frighten the toddler me of thunderstorms. Perhaps she feared them herself. Although I do not remember at all, Mom says Geraldine would exclaim with a sense of alarm, "Dark clouds, rain hard, Stevie; time to hide." Nor do I recall ever being frightened by lightning, thunder, ominous clouds, wind, or any other manifestation of nature's more threatening moods. Instead, Aunt Geraldine may have unintentionally ignited my lifelong love affair with weather, even adverse conditions.

I have a vague recollection (from sixty years ago) of sitting in my high chair, watching the sliver of sky that I could see through the kitchen window, rapidly (dizzyingly) transition from blue to very dark as clouds raced across. Even then, I puzzled over what I had seen. Nothing else emerges from the memory. Did a storm follow, or did the blue return? Perhaps Mom placed food in front of me, and the window view—with its curiously rapid cloud covering—slipped into a lower priority. Regardless, the memory is clear. I still puzzle over how nearly-instantaneously the clouds advanced. Given how much more deeply I now understand weather, I suppose that the visual memory is flawed or far too blurry to interpret. I observed and interpreted then through the visual and intellectual lenses of a three-year-old, and through those same lenses, stored the memory. How closely does what I recall seeing six decades later match the actual image visible through the parted curtain? The image I carry now is remarkable, like nothing I have seen since. I close my eyes, and the memory is vivid and real, yet it makes no sense through the perception of a sixty-five-year-old weather fanatic. What we see depends clearly on what tools, understanding, and knowledge we bring to the observation. And time adjusts the memory of what we see.

When I was a little older, yet still hand in hand with Dad, we walked through our streetlight-illuminated neighborhood during a snowstorm that Dad described as a blizzard. He had long before instructed me to extend an arm, palm perpendicular to my line of sight, shielding my eyes from the bare arc light, all the better to see the swirling sheets of wind-driven snow. We stood in silence enjoying the ever-shifting visual magic at every streetlight we passed. Dad recalled to me, as we walked that night, his experience of thunder-snow. I ache to remember what he said, but I cannot dredge it from memory. I've seen thunder-snow several times since, and I've manufactured a "memory" of the young boy seeing it with Dad. I opened my own children's eyes and hearts to the magic of shielding the bare light to better see and enjoy snow after dark. Now it's the grandchildren who will carry the magic forward. What we see gets filtered through an emotional lens. Our eyes see a simple dimension. Our heart, mind, soul, and spirit interpret with the language we call "magic." Do you look with just your eyes (body), or do you engage all five portals (body, heart, mind, soul, and spirit)?

I ran religiously for three decades, well into my forties, before joints complained too pitiably. My running logs recorded time, distance, effort, mood, routes, and weather conditions. One of these days, I will explore those chronicles to draw lessons from my own interplay of how I felt and the conditions in which I ran. Short of pulling out the journals and reading them, I can still recall some notable runs. We lived near Montgomery, Alabama during the early 1980s, the peak of my marathon-running stage. Because the kids were young and I devoted evenings to them, I usually ran pre-dawn.

Thirty years ago, I could not pull up the weather radar to preview conditions, cells, and their movement. One weekday midsummer, I left for a nine-mile round trip route, heading north on rural roads. Two miles out, with a clear view to the north, I saw lightning on the horizon. There was a narrow slice of a rain shield, illuminated every ten to fifteen seconds, just three to five degrees above the horizon. Still far enough away, I could not hear the thunder above my breathing and footfalls. It was still distant enough that I would not run headlong into the storm. I thought nothing of the beast, for storms in south-central Alabama almost always approach from the west or south. I ran the next ten to fifteen minutes through wooded countryside, the forests obscuring my view to the north. I could see the occasional non-point flash, and had begun to hear distant rumbles. I was still nonplussed. When I emerged into fields with a clear view to the north, I suddenly froze. The narrow visible rain shield and cloud base had climbed from horizon-anchored to some forty degrees or more above horizontal, stretching east-west as an advancing squall line. Frequent streaks of cloud-to-ground lightning quickened my heart. While I stood, the thunder reverberated deep in my chest and through my gut. This thing was galloping right at me, charging southbound through the darkness, and there I was four miles from home. I turned tail, knowing that I could not possibly outrun this early morning derecho.

I pushed hard. The breeze freshened and the thunder pounded. As the time between lightning and thunder closed to under five seconds (signifying it was one mile away), my fear merged with common sense. No country home in sight in which I could seek refuge on a porch, I slipped off the road shoulder to seek "shelter" in a roadside depression. Within seconds the wind howled, rain fell in torrents, and lightning popped much too close. I huddled—terrified, wet, and now cold. The fury soon passed to the south. Drenched and feeling out of harm's way, I regained the road and slogged home just as dawn began to brighten the eastern sky. I survived a bit worn and shaky from the experience, yet feeling a deep gratitude for the pleasurable terror. Had I known what I might encounter, I would not have ventured forth that morning. Having escaped harm, however, I felt absolute gratification and full reward for the experience. Was I near the jaws of death? Probably not. I had crouched low on all fours, as all "if-you-get-caught-by-such-a-storm" experts counsel. But I did absolutely feel full terror, thus sweetening the memory, and weaving it lucidly into the fabric of my life's journey.

I looked at the distant storm initially through the lens of experience—I "knew" it was moving from west to east, posing no threat to my morning ritual. Once I realized I was wrong, the reality of flight and fright kicked into high gear. I looked at the lightning, awakened with sharpened understanding, seeing the impending danger with new eyes. What we see depends on where we are. Both regrettably and blessedly, I did not need my flattened palm covering the arc light to see this storm.

Another thunderstorm holds a special place in memory. We were just a couple of years out of college, living in southeastern Virginia about an hour inland from Virginia Beach. A group of us chartered a weekend day of fishing offshore. It was a typical summer day, hot and humid, with a forecast for pop-up thundershowers, but nothing widespread or particularly ominous. We must have been at least a dozen miles out, catching some fish, enjoying beverages, and having a great time. In the late morning I watched the cumulus swell shoreward, and began to see some strong vertical development. After lunch, a few of them had structure and stature sufficient to draw the captain's attention, particularly one expanding column due west, building noticeably between us and where we had boarded that morning. He instructed us to haul in the gear, that we were heading back.

Within minutes of accelerating westbound, I watched the sky darken and deepen ahead of us, and knew that we would not avoid an encounter. The captain told us how to secure ourselves in this open-canopied vessel. Lightning flashed a constant warning. The wind, rain, and waves hit as one. A roar of nature's power amid the shameless screams and open prayers of some passengers, we all held tight to the boat and to each other. I was one with the storm, drawing in every dimension of sight, sound, feeling, and emotion, surprisingly unconcerned with the danger. Unlike the storm that years later interrupted my Alabama run, this one added the violent motion of fifteen to twenty foot waves. And like its terrestrial cousin, it quickly passed, leaving passengers soaked, cold, shaking, grateful, relieved, and some—acutely sea-sickened. I believe I drank another beer, watching the cell slip eastward, its vertical rear wall handsomely lit and glowing in the afternoon sun. Had I experienced the storm from a beachside hotel balcony, I would have enjoyed the show as a bystander, not as a participant. The vantage point makes all the difference in what we see as well as the mark left by the observation.

The late 1980s through mid-90s found us living in State College, PA, home of the Nittany Lions. I relished the four deep seasons, and watched winter patterns in hopes of an occasional coastal storm and deep central Pennsylvania snow. March 13, 1993 fell on a Saturday. The prior weekend The Weather Channel (TWC) and the National Weather Service had begun to foretell systems aligning to bring us a major storm the next weekend, typically far too soon to generate optimism or excitement for sating my storm-hunger. Yet the forecast both held and strengthened as we reached mid-week: a major storm with heavy snow and high winds loomed (or through my lens, "promised"). By Thursday morning, first a blizzard watch and then a blizzard warning headlined our forecast for Saturday. Thursday morning a fascinating bowling ball of energy and precipitation, clearly visible on composite radar and satellite loops, dipped from the western high plains into the Gulf of Mexico, and exploded within just a few hours. Possibility shifted to probability, and then certainty. I drooled in anticipation of the weather feast ahead.

The Storm of the Century, the Blizzard of '93, was alive and spinning, aiming for the mid-Atlantic coast at full strength! Friday reports from the Gulf, through the interior southeast, and the Carolinas evidenced that forecasts for us were on target. I hit the sack Friday night filled with anticipation. I recall awakening at 3:50, turning on the back deck light, and seeing the fine snow mist just beginning. A check of TWC radar confirmed that I awoke with the arrival of the precipitation's leading edge. Perhaps this was my sixth sense, confirmed many times in the course of my life; I have often awakened to approaching thunderstorms before the thunder is audible. The remainder of that Saturday was mine, focusing all my senses on the unfolding drama. I recall the major turning points:

- Judy and I walked the indoor track at Penn State about 7:00 AM. There were already a couple of inches of new snow, with intensity trending from light to moderate.
- By late morning, the snow fell at the rate of at least an inch per hour. I watched the breeze begin swirling spindrift from rooftops.
- After lunch the breeze had swelled to gale force, and snowfall rates exceeded two inches per hour.
- Midafternoon I found myself glued to the windows. The wind roared, I could not see the house across the street. Trained observers reported snowfall rates at five inches per hour. More than once I heard thunder.
- During that period I twice ventured out front, facing the lee, leaning back against the wind, all senses taut and intimately engaged. I enjoyed the storm as a participant, reveling in its beauty and fury. I embraced it and relished it, as an informed weather fanatic. I felt total humility and unbridled inspiration.

I saw nature's power bring the entire eastern US to a total standstill. I witnessed a fatal force bring a nation to its knees. I saw the indescribable beauty of wind-sculpted snow waves, corniced rooftops, and towering drifts. I understood that fury and beauty are two sides of the same coin. I welcome the occasional stark reminder of my own insignificance. I looked at the storm through informed and appreciative eyes. I did not feel the frustration, disruption, and inconvenience that filtered and dimmed what many others saw. I viewed magic, and power, and wonder. In fact, I see magic, power, wonder, beauty, inspiration, and awe even in the more subdued weather that graces our lives every day. Weather is one of nature's threads, perhaps the most palpable and tangible. Those threads weave the essence of the fabric of my life.

I recall driving my failing Dad into the central Appalachians sometime during his final year. Above twenty-five hundred feet elevation, deep snow mantled the fields and forests. Frozen rain from days before still glistened on all it had touched. Morning snow showers had added a fresh accumulation that now drifted across the road.

Dad and I connected via all five sensory portals that afternoon, palpably feeling, embracing, and reveling in the spirit of wonder and awe he had seeded and nourished in me many years prior. He told me then—his forty-five-year-old, second-born son, "You have been such a good boy." Dad still stands with me twenty years later whenever nature graces my days with beauty, awe, wonder, and magic. When, like this morning, snow falls before the dawn, my dad extends my arm, palm vertical, so I can relish the untamed flakes falling through the floodlights.

What we see depends entirely upon how we look, and the filters we employ: body, mind, heart, soul, and spirit. We are molded, and our vision is honed, by what we know and those who have touched us. I am my father's son, shaped by his touch. We can truly see only when we shield our eyes from the blinding source, and instead focus on what is illuminated.

CHAPTER EIGHT

Nature's Inspiration to Discover the Invisible

As the president of Antioch University New England (AUNE), I spoke to more than one hundred of our incoming students at their orientation in August 2015. I shared some of my philosophy about the university's approach to learning. I leveraged my early afternoon remarks with an experience from just that morning.

I left home at 7:00 AM, heading east toward Dublin School for the opening session of the Monadnock Conservancy annual meeting. So typical of late summer mornings, fog carpeted the hills and dales of southwestern New Hampshire. Pea soup fog filled the Ashuelot River valley in Keene, about ten miles east of my house, reducing visibility to near zero. By 7:30, the sun had begun to burn through the thick blanket. Climbing the hills east of Keene brought better visibility and an ever-brightening orb of sun, still mostly shrouded by the ground-hugging stratus. The air rich with moisture, dew adorned all surfaces. I peered intently into the foggy road ahead, and as visibility increased I began my usual pattern of also observing roadside nature. I keep an eye on my natural surroundings, always ready to appreciate and learn from nature.

My reward for paying attention that morning came suddenly and unforgettably, delivered through a visual gift from our natural world.

In retrospect, it was an absolute blessing. As I rounded a curve, ahead and inside to my left, a leafless, forty-five foot tall white birch stood along a fencerow, backlit by the emerging sun. I had rounded the same curve scores of times, not even conscious of seeing the lifeless form, the sentinel standing patiently as it awaited the pull of gravity playing on nature's slow decay. This morning, attributable to the special interplay of dew and light, hundreds of orb weaver webs graced the tree's barren limbs. Each geometric web was bejeweled and sparkling. The webs stood as the dominant image as I passed—magical in contrast to the stark, bare branches.

What was the lesson and gift for me? That heart-stopping image opened my eyes, literally and metaphorically. I realized that beauty, wonder, awe, and inspiration lie hidden within all things, and within all people. Hidden until special conditions reveal the invisible. I would not have seen the magic under any but these perfectly aligned conditions of heavy dew, thinning fog, and perfect backlighting. In fact, three hours later descending westward for the campus orientation I could not spot the tree, much less see what it had earlier revealed. That I could not locate the special tree after just a few hours deepened its memory imprint. I will never allow the image to fade. Writing these few words amount to permanent capture of the image and its translation into words.

I could think of little else as I drove back into Keene, the fog long since dissipated. You can guess the message I gave our new students. I told them of the morning journey, the thinning fog, the backlit tree, and its webbed splendor. I pledged to them that we, at this university, would hold fidelity to a critical responsibility: to assist them to discover through their graduate learning experience, the wonder, awe, beauty, magic, and inspiration that lie hidden within themselves as well as the world around them. We would encourage them to see the invisible, and carry it with them throughout life's journey. I suggested that only those who see the invisible can do the impossible. I saw the invisible that morning, and drew inspiration from it. The web-adorned, dead tree did not transcribe a lesson from nature. Instead, nature offered a scene from which I interpreted a lesson. Its simplicity proved magnificent and palpable.

I have reminded my colleagues and students over the years that we must first look if we hope to truly see. Only if and when we see, will we feel magic and inspiration. And only when we feel deeply will we be motivated and inclined to act. Critically, it is only through action that we make a difference. My role at the midday orientation was to welcome, inspire, and lift those adult incoming graduate students, to make them feel special. The morning's grand display made my remarks easy. They fit perfectly, and seemed to originate from a nature based spiritual force. Nature is replete with such germane lessons and inspiration. Only if we look, see, and feel deeply, will the lessons and inspiration make sense to us. Only if we are alert and accepting, will we add value to what we discover and interpret.

The AUNE Nature Based Leadership Institute is helping us learn lessons gleaned from nature—lessons for living, learning, serving, and leading. Nature based leadership defines and elaborates an approach to leadership steeped in the ways of nature. NBL borrows lessons from the ageless evolution of individual species and communities. Far more species have failed than survived over the vast sweep of time. Species often depend upon complex interrelationships within the community (ecosystem) they occupy and, in part, compose. Each species has a plan, hard wired in DNA. NBL identifies successful strategies and relationships, and extracts those that translate to enterprise applications that leaders can apply. NBL also leans heavily on nature's beauty, awe, wonder, and inspiration. NBL embraces tenets that can sustain the individual enterprise and assure Earth stewardship and human wellbeing. NBL implores and enables us to care for our common home and our fellow travelers.

Orb weaver spiders gain nothing from my appreciation of their webs in dew-bejeweled splendor. Instead, their webs serve them best, and perhaps only, when invisible to unsuspecting flying insects. For the spider, dew flashes a warning to potential prey, and may also furnish a sip of welcome hydration. Maybe, too, it offers a well-deserved rest for the vigilant predator.

Not long after that special morning I did spot the tree, barren and without a trace of magic. I marked its location mentally so I could easily monitor it with each subsequent passage. I've traveled the same route many times since, and watched for a repeat performance. Nothing beyond the bare, leafless skeleton has since emerged. In early March I drove past, noting that the tree no longer stood. Gravity, decay, and time prevailed, perhaps triggered by winter snow, ice, rain, and wind. No one will sound taps; future generations of orb weavers will find other aerial anchorage. As with all life, such wonder is fleeting and fragile. Those brief magic moments will reward us only if we stay alert to the special displays when conditions align. Likewise, as we deal with students, friends, colleagues, and others whose paths we share, we must watch for special conditions when we can help illuminate, incite, and appreciate the magic.

Good leaders see the magic and open blind eyes to the wonder and beauty that lie within. Nature withholds its secrets from those unwilling to look and see. I offer three examples of blindness.

First, one of the women on my staff at the University of Alaska Fairbanks shared a ride with me to Chamber of Commerce meetings downtown. A lifelong Fairbanks resident, she lamented the deep cold and darkness of winters at sixty-five degrees north latitude. To the contrary, I delighted in the magnificence that each day revealed. She saw only what her mind filtered; I saw what I chose to see. Midwinter, she opened her mind: "Steve, what a pleasure to see winter through your eyes." She still lives there. I have no idea whether she has re-imposed the glum winter filter. I hope not. Life is too short to filter beauty and magic from our intake portals. I reveled in Alaska's wonder. I rejoiced by filling heart, mind, body, soul, and spirit with all that the last frontier offered. I carry with me lessons and inspiration I shall always cherish.

The second example of blindness is what would happen when I

ventured so often into the natural environs during my twelve years of southern industrial forestry practice. The company owned more than two million acres across the six southeastern states. I would spend entire days traipsing through the woods, occasionally spotting a snake, but usually not. I didn't fear them, and actually enjoyed seeing them in their natural habitat. What bothered me a bit was that when I ventured into those southern forests with a colleague, that person (it did not matter which co-worker) would direct my attention to snakes all day long. From harmless black snakes to rattlers and moccasins. How many had I passed blithely during my solitary sojourns? Was my blindness exposing me to danger? I wondered, yet I did not feel concern. I watched carefully where I stepped. I paid attention to the forest, the lay of the land, and the site factors that influence forest operations. I inventoried and mapped as I paced and oriented. Perhaps not seeing snakes signaled that I was focusing where I should. Perhaps seeing snakes was a time-demanding luxury my workday could not afford or a distraction from the business at hand. Never once did a big viper strike my boot; I recall no close calls when I narrowly avoided stepping into a coiled canebrake rattlesnake.

What lesson might I draw from my paucity of snake encounters? Was I blind to them? Would I have seen them if they had been my primary focus? Was my snake blindness self-imposed? Maybe I emitted some aura that preceded me when alone—perhaps a bit of St. Patrick's magic. I think none of that. I believe I directed my attention otherwise. There are limits to what even those who look can see. I saw the forest in multiple dimensions. I could not see all facets. However, I occasionally enjoyed seeing my reptilian friends when a more astute observer accompanied me.

I offer a third brief example of blindness-turned-sight. I learned the art of imprinting when searching fields and other disturbed soil surfaces for Native American artifacts. A rain-washed arrowhead perched on the soil surface can be very difficult to spot ... until I would see the first one of the day. After that, the image was imprinted; my eyes (and head) knew what it was they sought, and subsequent artifacts would leap out at me. I suppose the lesson to us is to know what it is we seek. Whether arrowheads or deep life satisfaction, imprinting and visualization are essential. Otherwise, searching can be pointless, yielding little.

Nature based leadership is a type of imprinting. The more I look for and discover lessons in nature, the more nature reveals itself to me. Just as I triggered Ann's awareness in seeing the virtue in a Fairbanks winter, NBL enables the uninitiated to observe lessons and inspiration from nature through the eyes of those already aware. NBL removes filters and unclogs portals, permitting access to what nature has to offer. We will never see nature's lessons and inspiration unless we look, and we will see only if awareness through imprinting prepares us to translate a barren two-dimensional image to meaning. NBL opens new vistas, provides interpretative services, and offers lessons for life, education, service, and leadership. Life is drab and dull unless and until we imprint on it the beauty, awe, magic, and wonder hidden within. It will lie undisclosed until we choose to discover it. Nature holds the combination for unleashing the power and potential in what is too often unseen and unsought. NBL encourages and enables us to first look, and then imprint, see, and feel. Feeling deeply spurs action. And action can make tomorrow brighter.

CHAPTER NINE

Seeing the Invisible

The piece below (written in September 2011) predates the tale in the prior essay by four years, and comes before I began categorizing these thoughts and experiences as nature based leadership. I include it in this volume of essays as another example of how I have been noticing the magic and wonder of nature for many years.

Revelations come to us through circumstances often unheralded, revealing things hidden yet in plain sight. Bicycling the nearby rails to trail provides the opportunity to occasionally appreciate nature's divinations, both literal and symbolic. As summer yields to fall's abbreviated day-length, my schedule often forces me to the trail predawn. A week ago Saturday morning, during a weekend stacked with university events, brought me to the trail early. I left the house, just two hundred yards distance and thirty-five feet higher than the trail, at 5:30AM. All was well at the house, but I found thick fog draping the trail. I struggled to see, the fog's billions of microscopic droplets reflecting my very bright bicycle light and blinding me to what lay ahead. A mile later, my glasses coated to near-opacity and the fog no more penetrable, I turned back home. I was temporarily defeated but remained hopeful to squeeze in a few miles after daybreak.

I ventured out again after sunrise in thinning fog. I still had enough time to go out ten miles and return, moving at a good pace across the farmland punctuated with woodlots, field-edge trees, and riparian forests. The turnaround point brought lifted fog and full illumination. I've traveled this route scores of times. As an observer of nature, I know each field, stream, and wooded patch well; I thought I knew the landscape's secrets. As I exited a closed forest northbound, an eastside stretch of brush three to six feet tall under a power line displayed a scene of absolute beauty. Tens of thousands of orb-weaver webs, each thread a fog-droplet-jeweled strand backlit by the morning sun, decorated the brush with what seemed full interlocking brilliance. I slowed, and then stopped, astounded by a sight unexpected and unearned.

How many times in your life's journey have you encountered such wonder and splendor? How often has something invisible been revealed? As I pedaled homeward, I thought about the irony and symbolism embedded in this awakening of wonder. First, the predawn attempt thwarted by the blinding fog. Then my industrial-strength light that has unfailingly served me on my early rides, that morning actually impairing visibility in the fog. Each of us has occasionally suffered when the familiar is blurred and distorted by conditions of the moment. When the light (intellectual, emotional, and/or spiritual) that normally illuminates and reveals, ends up obscuring our vision, insight, and understanding. That morning I found myself lost on my own turf in what is otherwise a zone of absolute comfort: the nearby trail.

Later, with the rising sun and lifting haze, I discovered that the very agent of blindness (the morning's fog) had actually brought clear definition and full visibility to the unseen, unknown, and unanticipated. Without the fog, I would have pedaled blindly day in and day out past the right-of-way, never knowing the delicate magic of the dew-dropped webs, nor even suspecting the true complexity and nature of the brush field. It also struck me that what I saw as beauty stands as a deadly gauntlet to the flying insects seeking passage. Ironic, too, that like much in nature, beauty and danger share the same space and time.

I ventured forth again the next day in the midmorning, passing the brushy right-of-way and seeing nothing of particular interest, until I stopped. The webs remained but, without their trimmings, had resumed their intended obscurity. Our lives slip past with so much of potential interest and importance shielded from our too shallow and terribly distracted senses and attention. Some things we choose not to see; others are hidden by the pressures that seem to force us too quickly along the trail.

There is great reward in seeing that which we usually pass by. This time of year in central Ohio the first heavy frost of the season is not too far away. The chilly morning warrants close attention, which most of us don't give it. Because frost rarely accompanies cloudy skies, we can expect the sun to guild the crisp landscape with dazzling beauty on a grand scale. The aesthetic is incomparable; the symbol of what lies ahead is powerful. Appreciating the frosted grass on a mesoscale only deprives us of the magnificent image of a frosted grass blade under even minimum magnification. Take a magnifying glass outdoors and examine the intricate design and three-dimensional grace. A single blade of frosted grass is sure to make you feel rather small. I think, too, of other routine elements of our daily existence that we casually ignore in the bustle of our passage. Here are a few that carry great meaning and joy for me: snow on barren branches, a smile on the face of a friend, joyful tears of a loved one, a familiar voice in song, a child's laughter.

Don't wait for the fog to clear; lift yourself above the distractions that dull and diminish life. Slow down and take a closer look. Watch for the clarity that can come from unanticipated moments. Be aware: anticipate and observe. Learn to see and appreciate what makes the passage worth the effort.

Nature based leadership instructs us to seek the beauty, awe, magic, and wonder that lie within all things and all people. The Nature Based Leadership Institute spurs us to learn from nature, draw inspiration from nature, and act responsibly to care for the earth in all that we do. Seeing what lies hidden within deepens our understanding that nature is an intricate web, that we are one with the intimate interdependence not separate from it. NBL reminds us of our obligation to tend all elements of the whole that is nature.

Whether biking the trail, walking to lunch, playing with the kids, sitting on a park bench, or exploring a new business partnership, we know from NBL that jeweled beauty lies tucked within. Inspiration and revelation are there for our discovery. All it takes is for us to look, to see, to feel, and to act on those deep feelings.

Living, learning, serving, and leading involve far more than going through the motions, mechanically and blindly. Simply pedaling, covering the miles, and journaling the exercise do not constitute a journey. It's a good cardio workout but not a rewarding adventure. Life is a journey, not a sordid mechanical exercise. NBL urges us to use all of our powers of receptivity in every aspect of that journey. Unless we do, we miss the sparkling webs of life's journey.

As We Grow Older

A Guest Essay by Craig Cassarino

As we grow older, reflection starts to become an intrinsic part of our lives. Lately, I have been reflecting on how nature has taught me how to live.

Recently, I helped coordinate a meeting at the Nature Based Leadership Institute, where the focus was on using nature as healer to serve our military veterans with emotional and physical issues. At the end of the introductions, someone commented that all seven of us at the table had mentioned the importance of natural environments to our childhood well-being and development, and to determining who we are now.

My reflection to the group was about how I spent the summers from 1950-57 in the woods of southern New Hampshire with my grandfather. Gramps was a teamster, however not of the union kind. He worked a team of horses, Tom and Queenie. I helped him as he yarded logs, working many hours outside each day. Today, when I walk into the woods and smell pine sap or pass a sweating horse, it brings me back to those days. Those summer experiences merged the human, animal, and ecosystems, which taught me harmony, compassion, empathy, and how important diversity was. I had learned how to take comfort from nature.

Another formative period for me was from 1967-72 when Dr. Avery Johnson and Dr. Warren Brody, introduced me to the word "ecology." Avery and Warren mentored me, showing me "possibilities." For the first time, I realized that everything is connected, and self-organizing. Nature was again my teacher. Ecological systems thinking has become part of everything I do. Systems and feedback loops allow me to connect the dots for business and life.

That I could use nature's lessons to guide me became clearer as I trusted its principles. Several crucial experiences contributed to my progress, including: attending Antioch University, living in Brazil for five years, founding Leonardo Technologies Inc., meeting my wife, and having a son. I learned how to be a father, a husband, a businessman while creating a sense of living in place within my community and my personal ecosystem.

A few years ago an important event happened: I met Steve Jones. He suggested that it was "correspondence" that brought us together. I immediately felt a kinship, like I was coming home. Our early childhoods were not dissimilar. We had taken different paths and yet ended up in the autumn of our years coming to some of the same conclusions. Steve expressed his journey, reflections, and values to me in such a way that I understood our meeting was no coincidence. He saw something in me that I had missed in my own self-evaluations over the past seventy-two years. Our connection was empowering, collaborative, spiritual, and regenerative. It inspired me to blend and balance nature's lessons in a transformative way. Steve Jones and the Nature Based Leadership Institute have given me the energy and courage to continue to lead our fight for social and environmental justice.

Bio

Mr. Cassarino is the Executive Director of the Alianca Foundation. Craig lives In Amherst, New Hampshire with his wife Cleatia, son Caio and two dogs. He and his family enjoy tending their herd of Grass Fed Akaushi Beef Cattle. Craig was instrumental in the formation of Leonardo Technologies, Inc., incorporated in 2001, and currently sits on the Board of Directors. His appointment from the State of New Hampshire as Commercial Consul to Brazil has allowed him to develop projects in Brazil, which focus on Sustainable Development and Regenerative Agriculture. He is a founding member of the Nature Based Leadership Institute. He received a Master's of Science Degree in Resource Management and Conservation from Antioch New England University.

CHAPTER TEN

Winter Mount Washington Summit Attempt

A ntioch University New England alumnus Will Broussard, Master of Science in Environmental Studies with a concentration in Conservation Biology, is Outreach Coordinator at the Mount Washington Observatory in North Conway, NH. Mount Washington, with a summit at over sixty-two hundred feet, reports some of the "world's worst weather." Will hosted my wife Judy and me several summers ago when we visited the observatory and the Extreme Mount Washington Museum. "Breathtaking" describes both the museum and our summit experience. Will invited me to return for a winter visit. So in February of the following year, Will drove me from the headquarters in North Conway to the snowcat garage at the base of the Mount Washington auto road, closed during the long winter season.

We boarded the snowcat, a powerful tracked vehicle with its heated ten-passenger cab and hydraulic plow blade, at 9:30 AM for the ascent. Breezy and zero degrees at the base, the summit observers reported sixty mph winds and minus eighteen, with a forecast of intensifying gusts up to one hundred mph and further dropping temperatures by early afternoon. We could see the spindrift racing across the Presidential Range's upper slopes; clouds capped the summits. A series of lenticular clouds eight to ten miles downwind evidenced the powerful winds.

The scene spurred our excitement for entering the alpine zone and experiencing a bit of extreme weather.

We enjoyed the rumbling, vibrating ride through the northern hardwood forest which transitioned with the elevation to spruce, which gradually gave way to spruce shrub cover. Entering the shrub zone introduced the gusting wind and blowing snow, which yielded as we climbed to a howling gale and near-whiteout. The open tundra that followed exposed us fully to hurricane force winds and nearly continuous whiteout in the ground blizzard. A state park tracked plow had led our snowcat to this point, slowing often as it pushed through deeper and deeper drifts. We stopped and disembarked to experience the conditions as well as to give the plow a chance to gain some distance. I wore my Alaska arctic gear, leaving no skin exposed. This proved to be the worst winter weather I had seen or felt in my entire life. Nature's fury leaves no doubt about its dominance over us. I felt humility in its teeth, and inspiration as I glanced at the tremendous heights still above us.

Returning to the cab, we continued our journey. We stopped at a turnout clearing to await the state park plow, which reported by radio that it had encountered impossible conditions not far ahead. We again disembarked to feel the fury. The wind threw one of our traveling companions to the ground. I fought to keep my feet.

The state park plow passed by us on its descent, stopping briefly to report the conditions to our driver, who then advised us that we, too, would head back to the base. He suggested that before returning we walk to a point several hundred feet ahead where we could see what brought us to a halt. The wind buffeted us as we rounded a curve. We saw where the plow had stopped; a wall of snow marked the terminus. Huge drifts lay ahead as far as we could see during brief lulls in the ongoing whiteout. We struggled to walk. Blowing snow almost immediately obscured our footprints, and rapidly-growing drifts had begun filling in behind the departed plow.

We failed to summit, forced to turn at fifty-three hundred feet by ferocious winds, a total whiteout, and drifts up to ten feet blocking the road. The air temperature stood at negative ten with a wind chill of fifty below. Observers at the summit reported temperatures more frigid than minus twenty, with winds gusting above a hundred mph, and a wind chill approaching negative eighty! I would have been disappointed had we turned with just marginal conditions. However, we faced an easy decision; from that point upward, we would have been in severe peril. Good sense prevailed.

Once again in my life's journey, the twin lessons of humility and inspiration imparted wisdom for living, learning, and leading. As I braced with my back to the wind and my senses sharpened by the sight, sound, feel, and fury, I could only imagine what it must have been like at the higher altitudes. That we occupy such a hostile environment around the clock at the Mount Washington Observatory for the sake of science and learning is testimony to our hunger for knowing more and more about our place on this Earth. Yes, we failed to summit, but we did not fail to learn. The lesson: that we are not apart from nature; we are one with nature.

Perhaps one day by understanding the extremes we can better live sustainably within the calmer zones we inhabit. We must remember that this land sustains us. Acting otherwise places us at ultimate peril. Let nature's extremes remind us of our vulnerability and of our obligation to informed Earth stewardship.

I encouraged embedding this "one with nature" lesson in the fabric of Antioch University New England's Nature Based Leadership Institute, and sharing this tale for the benefit of those engaged and for the many we hope to touch. All lessons distill to stories. I will take my Mount Washington summit attempt to the end of my life's journey, telling and retelling my story and the simple, yet essential, lesson conveyed and embraced.

Will Broussard's role as Outreach Coordinator at the observatory provides him with a wonderful opportunity for sharing such lessons and reminders with everyone he reaches, young and old, through his education efforts. Each person he persuades and informs represents a step toward ensuring a brighter tomorrow, and stands as one more potential victory for humanity. Our graduates inspire me, and assure me that I am where I belong.

I am grateful for the chance to attempt the ascent, experience what Robert McGrath described as nature's "pleasurable terror," and to return comfortably to the base.

CHAPTER ELEVEN

Successful Mount Washington Winter Ascent

Every time I venture into nature I learn. The deeper I go, the tendency for deeper learning. Nature rewards looking, encourages seeing, inspires feeling, and spurs action. Try leading without these; such practice leads to an empty promise, a failed exercise. This essay explores some of the deeper perception and learning that came from my subsequent winter ascent (two years later) of New Hampshire's Mount Washington with a group of friends and colleagues. Once again, we took advantage of the observatory's snowcat, and its scheduled resupply and shift change round trip from base.

On St. Patrick's Day, we arrived at the Mount Washington Observatory (MWO) base employee lot at 8:10 AM. This time we enjoyed forty-five degree temperatures, occasional sprinkles, breezes, and bare ground. We parked facing the summit, which was obscured above four thousand feet by its cloud cap, and awaited our ride to the operations center. Clouds raced from the southwest, allowing shafts of morning sun to penetrate, briefly spotlighting random side slopes. We watched mountain-clinging clouds forming in lifting air and dissipating downslope, as the wind found its way around and over the irregular terrain.

We left the operations center garage about forty-five minutes later in one of the MWO vans, driving up to the snowcat that was parked two miles out. Even there, winter's residual snow did not fully cover the auto road surface. We boarded the snowcat, following the van for another two miles, where we would park the cat when we descended midafternoon. Beyond the four-mile point (at four thousand feet), packed snow covered the road to the summit. The prior night's precipitation had fallen there as wet snow, coating the sparse vegetation windward, dripping now at slightly above freezing. Another five hundred feet elevation took the temperature below freezing. Above that, the night's dry snow had blown and drifted. We had re-entered winter, leaving spring below. Visibility in dense, wind-driven fog had fallen to a few dozen feet, flattening depth in a grey world.

Well above the prior February's terminal fifty-three hundred foot elevation (and the dangerous conditions that forced us to abandon our ascent), we could see nothing. I asked one of our MWO hosts whether we were yet on the leg appropriately named The Home Stretch. Will Broussard, with us again this ascent, gestured through the window at the building caked in rime ice that was just emerging from the grey obscurity outside. We had summited! Our cat driver plowed a spot in the lee-of-the-building snowdrifts. We parked, disembarked, and entered.

Weather nerds (I am admittedly of the ilk) thrive on the kind of anticipation that day's forecast held for the summit. Midday frontal passage, cold upper air pocket, lots of vertical energy combining to trigger thunder snow: a wild, dynamic atmosphere. For the moment, it was twenty-five degrees with zero visibility, light and blowing snow, wind sustained at forty mph, accumulating rime ice, and the radar showing a few convective returns beginning to bubble.

Inside the center we stowed our gear and planned the next several hours. The operations hub in the parapet greeted us with the aroma of homemade cinnamon rolls wafting from the kitchen below. We followed our noses down the spiral staircase. Volunteers nourished us with the oven-fresh delicacies and fresh coffee. Not only had we summited, we had entered the kingdom of heaven! MWO volunteers are angels of the heights.

Our Antioch contingent and key MWO hosts sequestered ourselves in a conference room for strategic collaboration. Sure, we could have conducted business by phone. The hour and a half we had just enjoyed face-to-face, ascending into the clouds, surrounded by the mountain's beauty and harshness, provided inspiration and stimuli that simply do not translate through phone lines. We laid bare our hopes and shared vision, a cogent plan that we have since drafted into a memorandum of agreement. MWO and AUNE share a lot of DNA. We knew we could do things together that neither institution could accomplish in isolation. We owe much of our insight and outcome to the mountain.

We once again visited the volunteers for a typical March 17th meal of corned beef, cabbage, and potato soup as reward for our intense planning. The radar now depicted an intense squall line charging eastward from Vermont, threatening (or, promising—for the storm enthusiasts) some wild summit conditions within the hour. We were advised to hurry along with our final tour elements, don our gear, visit the deck, and head to the snowcat. Visibility remained at zero, the wind gusting to sixty at the deck railing. Two to four inch rime feathers grew into the wind, a direction of growth that at first seems so counterintuitive. We encountered knee-high to waist-high drifts as we trekked the short distance to the snowcat. We once more stashed our gear and boarded.

Five hundred feet below the summit we glanced back up to see the observatory emerge in full detail, momentarily escaping its grey bondage. Sorry that we were not still there, we could see ominous darkness behind it to the west as the line neared. Below the cap-cloud base we could see numerous convective cells north and east of us. Now below the freezing line, we could discern the snow to rain transition in the vertical profile under each cell. The dense greyish white of snow faded to less opaque curtains of rain. Our wipers cleared the windows of rain. Several in our party saw a flash of lightning over Mount Adams to our north.

The squall line hit as we rushed into the base service center. The gusts delivered heavy rain and snow pellets. Each of us wondered what the line had delivered at the summit. Would we have witnessed the much anticipated thunder snow? Would the storm have delayed our descent? Perhaps it would have fallen short of the imagined ferocity. The answer came to me via email four days later, when MWO meteorologist Tom Padham shared the hourly summaries and point-in-time special notes from the summit on the day we'd been there. We left the summit a little before 2:00. The weather notes I reviewed later reported a thunderstorm from 2:14 to 2:30 with heavy snow and blowing snow. Hourly wind observations at 2:00 and 3:00 depicted only the steady thirty-five to forty mph.

Tom elaborated that the hourly observations missed the thunderstorm action, "During the thunderstorm winds doubled, going from approximately thirty-five mph to a peak gust of seventy-three mph in only a few minutes. We had three direct lightning strikes to the summit, with plenty of excitement amongst the staff at the first flash as it meant a thunderstorm had officially begun. There were two other rounds of heavier, more convective (though not thunderstorm) showers during the remainder of the afternoon and early evening, with similar increases in wind speed including the peak gust of the day at eighty-three mph." Tom added another element that made our trip all the more special, "Thunderstorms only occur approximately twenty days out of the year on the summit, with the vast majority of these occurring during the summer months." So, it's confirmed. We did it again: we enjoyed an unusual day on the mountain!

When we aborted our prior ascent due to horrendous conditions, I had no trouble drawing conclusions and finding seminal and indelible lessons for living, learning, serving, and leading. Failure teaches many lessons. That we successfully summited this year forced me into more exhaustive introspection. The conclusions and reflections surfaced less easily, yet they did emerge. In fact, I am grateful for the incremental labor, and for the wonderfully wild day. I relish the reward in satisfaction and fulfillment. The yield—some inspired conclusions and observations.

Conclusions

My psyche vibrates in resonance with forecast weather extremes. I sleep restlessly in advance of storms—not in fear, dread, or trepidation, but with the anticipated thrill of experiencing the predicted adverse (by other people's standards) conditions. Awaiting the arrival, I wake often, heart racing and adrenalin coursing. Such was the case Thursday morning, first driving to the base, and then wending our way up the road. Is this a throwback to ancient hardwiring evolved from our need then to be more consciously one with nature?

My pulse quickened even as we sat in the employee lot. Every view evidenced high atmospheric energy, a condition that inspires the weather dweeb in me. I could have sat for hours, mesmerized by the constant motion and unending patterns, each begging explanation and interpretation. I am at comfort with nature's patterns; the human environment puzzles and confuses me far more deeply.

Dynamic atmospheric mixing brings magic to the sky—racing clouds and deepening convection, along with wonderfully mixed light and shadows. From the parking lot until the cloud cap swallowed us, the poetry and symphony of movement entertained and inspired me. I thought of Robert Noyes' "The Highwayman": "The wind was a torrent of darkness among the gusty trees; the moon was a ghostly galleon tossed upon cloudy seas." Even his words weave a tapestry of magical orchestration. I confess to drifting off during performances when I served on a symphony board in Ohio; never has nature's dynamic orchestration lulled me to sleep. I can close my eyes now and relive Thursday's complex chords.

This mountain spurs deep spirituality in me. I feel closer to something far greater than myself, whether religious or secular. I departed Mount Washington once more accepting absolute humility and feeling full inspiration. A healthy balance: a reminder that each of us is simply a cog in a far greater system (or a business, a family). We are mere moments across the vast sweep of time. The mountain will stand high for millennia, long after I have passed. MWO's Brian Fowler emailed me the Sunday after our ascent, sharing similar sentiments: "Well, you now know one of the principal reasons I stay connected with the observatory. Once it gets into your blood (for me now almost fifty years ago), it's there permanently and always available as a wonderful palliative to this otherwise perplexing world."

My Antioch colleagues, Melinda Treadwell and Jim Gruber, and I shared a magnificent day on the mountain. We are immeasurably stronger and closer for it, teammates bonded by the experience. Our shared adventure—especially one so magical in the teeth of environmental extremes and incomparable raw beauty—unified us with each other and with our MWO hosts.

I've occasionally experienced tremendous negative dynamism and organizational swirling along my career journey. I contrast that to the fury of purpose and beauty we weathered on the mountain. Every last perturbation holds meaning, every movement of the symphony explained by natural forces seeking balance and release. Too often within an enterprise, fury is absent logic, explanation, and purpose. The winds howl, the organization suffers, casualties result, nothing is gained, few lessons are learned. Why can't we take the time to understand the rules, discover the forces at play, and learn how to conduct the orchestra?

Unfortunately, organizational tumult fails to inspire. Its chaos carries no beauty. Purpose evades all but the most circumspect. And unlike our willing, even eager, entry to Thursday's dynamic swirling, organizations fall into the chaos involuntarily, not realizing they have entered the maelstrom until it's too late to avoid it. Many entities do not survive. They fail to escape the conditions even when leadership radar is signaling the approaching squall line. Those leaders are not looking, and they surely are not seeing what should be obvious. Failing to see, they escape the feeling of woe and apprehension of what lies ahead. And the absence of feeling and awareness delays necessary action. The leader who fails to act, simply fails. Our dear Jedi Master Yoda once observed that there is "do," and there is "not do." There is no "try to do." I remind you that nature does not bother with trying. Nature only does. Nature based leadership demands that we pay attention. Thursday on the mountain reminded me that nature rewards looking, encourages seeing, inspires feeling, and spurs action.

Had the day been clear, we could have seen the summit from the service garage, eight miles by road and perhaps five by line of sight. It's sobering to think that such proximity yields the extremes we experienced. From bare ground, light breeze, and mid-forties to drifting snow, rime ice, zero visibility, punishing winds, and mid-twenties. Is there an embedded nature based lesson for leadership? Yes, our enterprise-operating environment can change quickly with minute distances and abbreviated time. What we see where we stand in place and time is not static. The five-mile differences between base and summit, quite fortunately, are predictable and measurable. Such is not always the case for leadership. However, the more we understand our operating environment the better we can anticipate shifts and perturbations. Leaders must seek to understand and anticipate. For a hiker attempting to summit Mount Washington, an eight-mile walk could have proven deadly. Such fate awaits careless leaders and unprepared enterprises.

Again, nature offers lessons for those willing to look, see, feel, and act. We established the Antioch University New England Nature Based Leadership Institute to examine how leaders can learn from nature's lessons.

"On the tops of mountains, as everywhere to
hopeful souls, it is always morning."
Henry David Thoreau

CHAPTER TWELVE

Soil Nourishes All Life

R on Dodson—longtime friend, colleague, wildlife biologist, sustainability author, scholar, and speaker—asked me this spring via email, "From a leadership perspective (The Nature of Leadership), can you make a case for understanding the importance of soil and its position in regard to sustainability as a good starting point for fostering leadership development?" Ron asks some tough questions! I will attempt an answer.

I think we all know what soil is. It's the weathered surface layer that supports life. Although soil is rich in fauna, we commonly think of soil as the medium where plants sink their roots. From the soil, plants secure anchorage and draw water, nutrients, and essential gases.

My doctoral dissertation is titled, "Evaluation of Soil-Site Relationships for Allegheny Hardwoods." I studied the influence of soil and related topographic features on the forest. Since completing and earning the PhD in 1987, I have occasionally thought of myself as a soil scientist. For the past twenty years, I have been a university administrator who used to be a soil scientist, yet the old discipline still stirs within, reminding me that all life is rooted on the earth, and in the earth (soil) that characterizes, enables, and limits life and terrestrial ecosystems globally and locally.

Soil is such a great metaphor for individuals and human enterprises.

It is a living substrate, an artifact of bedrock, climate, living organisms, topography, and time. It's a substrate of mineral particles, organic matter, moisture, and air, teeming with roots, fungi, and microbes diverse and abundant. The living components shape the soil; concomitantly, the soil is architect of the living community within it. The relationship is one of complementarity, reciprocity, integration, and absolute interdependence.

The soil is shelter and sustenance. It is both anchorage for vascular plants and feeding trough for whatever multifaceted living community it supports. The plant cover in turn protects the soil from the incessant power of raindrop impact, even as the soil absorbs and retains the deluge that would otherwise erode and wash it ocean-ward. The deal between soil inhabitants (whether microbes or Sequoias) is ironclad, shaped by the ages. We are all soil-dependent, whether that is obvious to us or not.

We ignore this soil-dependence at our peril. Soil is the fundamental medium of the world.

This One Earth is our mote of dust in the vast darkness of space. No one from without will come to rescue us from ourselves. Pope Francis implored us to wake up before we cross a frightening threshold.

All enterprises depend upon leaders tapping a substrate, characterized as diversely as soil, shaped by a metaphorical suite of parent material, climate, living organisms, topography, and time. The leadership soil consists of knowledge, wisdom, experience, ethics, character, motivation, ethos, attitude, environment, teamwork, service, values, spirit, emotion, inspiration, and so much more. Likewise, the quality of leadership depends on the relative proportion and abundance of these and other constituents. Poor leadership soil yields inferior results. Rich and deep leadership soil provides firm anchorage and high productivity. Soil comes in nearly infinite variations. So too does leadership. I've spoken of the chance an oak takes when it drops an acorn and expects it to find just the right spot—courtesy of gravity, luck, squirrel, jay, or crow.

What shapes our individual and enterprise soils? And how does that nourish us?

Nature based leaders need not rely upon gravity, luck, squirrel, jay, or crow. Nature based leaders create their own medium, and fashion a substrate of their choosing. I recall the mission statement we created at NC State when we established the Shelton Leadership Center: "To inspire, educate, and develop values-based leaders committed to personal integrity, professional ethics, and selfless service." The mission has not changed over the dozen years since then. Clearly—as I reflect today upon that mission—I see the nature based metaphor of the soil we wanted leaders to seek, prepare, and depend upon. We encouraged leaders then, and I do now, to live by bedrock ideals, to embrace professional ethics, and to serve selflessly. Doing so, in turn, protects and buffers that substrate from the torrents and vagaries of day-to-day enterprise life that might otherwise wash the leadership soil to the metaphorical sea.

So in living, learning, serving, and leading, leaders shape and are shaped by the substrate that sustains them. One element of that leadership soil must be fidelity to our individual and collective obligation to responsibly steward this one Earth, and to tend the earth soil that sustains all life and every enterprise. Nature based leadership reminds us that our roots must find anchorage and sustenance, and that our relationship to our enterprise's substrate (and our earth soil) is fully one of complementarity, reciprocity, integration, and absolute interdependence. Sustainability relies upon our relationship with the applicable medium (whether earth soil or enterprise soil). We are one with nature, even as we are one with our own individual and enterprise nature.

Finally, human population now stands at nearly eight billion. Too many of us live empty lives—unfulfilled and only marginally purposed—from birth through final passage. We are not tending our soil. Collectively, as an Earth society we are lost, wandering aimlessly and ravaging the very nature and soil that sustain us. Nevertheless, we humans are blessed with remarkable abilities: intelligence, the capacity to love, an animate body, spirit, and soul. We have the metaphorical senses to look, see, feel, and act. And we must act now before we topple over the abyss. We will not act unless we feel deeply about the cause and its urgency. We will not feel unless we see the need—deeply and emphatically. We will not see unless we look for the peril that escapes our societal blindness. We need to begin now to systematically remove the blinders, open eyes, inspire vision, generate deep feelings, and motivate action—to tend our soil of earth and individual nature.

Ask yourself, "What quality is your life's soil? Your enterprise soil? Are you doing your part to tend the soils that sustain you … and us?" I urge you to look for where we, and you, are falling short. Truly see what is at stake. Feel deeply the consequences of neglecting our obligation to the soil. To act on its behalf in service to all, and to all who will follow.

Nature based leadership reminds us that nothing is truly distinct from nature, either actually or symbolically. Nature offers limitless lessons and unfathomable inspiration. We've created the Nature Based Leadership Institute to document those lessons that are directly applicable to our lives, our aspirations, our service. And we are chronicling the kind of inspiration that only effective leaders model—inspiration borrowed shamelessly from nature.

Ecotone: Convergence of Inner/ Outer Landscapes

A Guest Essay by Jennifer J. Wilhoit

I live, learn, serve, and lead by many of the NBL tenets mentioned in this book. I view my ever-deepening relationship to nature and its lessons through various ecological concepts; this brief essay will touch on just one: ecotones. Simply, an "ecotone" is a transition area between two biomes—like where a forest meets a meadow. When I first encountered this term, I fell instantly and abidingly in love. I inherently understood the potency of an ecotone, biologically and symbolically. I immediately sensed that I had come home—to this earth, to myself, and to the diverse community of beings who inhabit this planet.

Living: Edge

An ecotone is an edge place that joins two or more distinct biological communities. From preferring to sleep alone outside as a toddler... to researching, writing about, abiding in nature on seven continents throughout adulthood...I have craved edge places. My life is characterized by what I call the "inner/outer landscape": a dynamic interrelationship between experiences in my internal life and intimacy with the natural world. Thoughts, emotions, spirituality join with flora, fauna, landscapes, and weather in the ecotone of experience. Nature's ecotones reflect the diversity, complexity, cycles, wildness, and friendliness of human nature.

Learning: Biodiversity

An ecotone is especially bio-diverse because it contains species from each natural area that converges there. The learning I have pursued is also richly diverse: wilderness rites of passage, courses, trainings, scholarly research. My graduate work in interdisciplinary ecological studies included the arts, people-park conflicts, educational philosophy, and environmental justice; it is as rich in diversity as the species converging in an ecotone. What I've learned about and from nature extends beyond the cognitive to include spiritual insight, emotional intelligence, bodily knowing.

Serving: Transition

Ecotones are transition areas. I have served my community for four decades as a trained volunteer in myriad capacities. For the last fifteen years my volunteerism has focused on hospice, serving the dying and grief transitions associated with physical passing. A nature based perspective in hospice work reminds us that we are members of the community of all living beings. Nature models—in ebbing tides, falling leaves, or decaying detritus—the normalcy and ease of dying.

Leading: Niche

An ecotone is the niche for some highly adaptable species that thrive in its abundance. My professional work supports others' deep story processes. I guide people through inner/outer landscapes via writing, nature and creative experiences, life transition support, and mediation. My mentorship supports clients' exploration of their preferred habitat: self-awareness, wholeness, community, and meaningful work. They adapt, viewing life's turning points as opportunities to thrive. I have found my niche as a nature based leader in a multidisciplinary practice guiding people home to their inner/outer landscapes.

My life, personal and professional, is informed by, impassioned through, and sustained by nature's realities and metaphors. I live intertwined with ecotones of the inner/outer landscape—vibrant edges where human inner experience meets the wild beauty of nature.

Bio

Jennifer J. Wilhoit is a spiritual ecologist and the founder of *TEALarbor stories* (www.tealarborstories.com). She earned her PhD in Environmental Studies (people-park conflicts at the edges of protected areas, especially between crafts coops and conservationists), and her MA in Education (environmental, intercultural adult learning). She works as a published author, editor, writing mentor, life guide, mediator, speaker, trainer, educator, researcher, and hospice volunteer. She replenishes herself through hiking, building nature altars, photography, reading, collage and painting, travel, and playing in a carillon choir. Jennifer thrives in the beautiful Pacific Northwest landscape in which she lives.

CHAPTER THIRTEEN

The Peregrine Falcon

otems, omens, signs, talismans. What do they mean? Do they help or hinder our understanding of place, meaning, or context? Do they assist us in anticipating what lies ahead? Do they comfort or bode ill? Do they have a place in guiding or illuminating decision-making or leadership? Do they introduce yet another set of leadership lessons from nature? I cannot definitively answer these questions. Yet, I can reflect on my personal experience when one such "sign" appeared to me, and how I sought insight, wisdom, and solace from it.

Though six months ago, the memory is vivid and lasting. I had arrived early for an airport hotel interview within sight of Atlanta's Hartsfield. In fact, I had four hours to kill. Forced to book either a flight leaving no cushion between arriving and the scheduled interview, and arriving earlier with a much longer buffer, I chose the latter. I don't do well with cutting it close, so there I was. Fortunately, I had a special frequent-guest relationship with that hotel chain; they permitted me access to their executive lounge.

A major winter storm then spinning off the New Jersey coast had powered through the southeastern USA the night before my arrival. The rain in Atlanta had transitioned to snow before tapering off, leaving a few patches on grass where it had stuck. Now on the storm's backside, punishing northwest winds carried flurries and occasional snow showers, an unusual sight in Atlanta, Georgia—even in mid-January.

I had just missed a departing hotel shuttle at the terminal. Standing in the horizontal snow flurries, I found buffer from the wind in one of those three-sided glass bus shelters. My suit jacket interview garb made the fifteen-minute wait seem much longer. A strong bus heater and subsequent delivery to the hotel entrance warmed my body. However, I felt a bit cold mentally and emotionally to the whole idea of even being there. I already had a rewarding job, with much yet to accomplish, yet a disturbing trend at higher levels within my institution spurred me to consider this particular opportunity. My wife of decades, had said, "The time is not right. The potential position is not right for us." I was in Atlanta anyway, against her better judgment and instincts, which over many years had served us well. Nevertheless, I felt a growing unease with the current position.

The executive lounge looked south from the seventeenth floor. FedEx's Atlanta operations spread out beneath us, the commercial airport beyond that. I could hear and feel the wind swirling around the building, even on this sheltered lee side. Making myself at home, I pulled out my laptop, secured connectivity, and went about conducting the business of the university that employed me, occasionally revisiting my notes and background materials for the interview. Peripherally, I noticed a fellow lounge occupant near the window, camera in hand. I rose to see the object of her attention. There on the eight-inch-wide window ledge more than one hundred fifty feet above the ground stood a peregrine falcon.

The Cornell Lab of Ornithology website describes the bird. "Powerful and fast-flying, the peregrine falcon hunts medium-sized birds, dropping down on them from high above in a spectacular stoop. They were virtually eradicated from eastern North America by pesticide poisoning in the middle twentieth century. After significant recovery efforts, peregrine falcons have made an incredible rebound and are now regularly seen in many large cities and coastal areas." I think of the peregrine as a majestic bird of prey.

The morning gale had obviously buffeted my window ledge falcon. Although now somewhat protected, feathers still in disarray, the bird evidenced its wind-bludgeoning.

My dominant initial impression of the bird, within arm's length beyond the glass, filtered through my own lens as an unabashed champion of accipiter species and other birds of prey, amounted to wonder, awe, beauty, and inspiration. I did not contemplate its ruffled feathers at first, only marveled that this incredible bird had suddenly appeared on such a blustery morning on my seventeenth floor ledge! Only later when viewing peregrine photos online did I truly appreciate how bedraggled this one looked.

Regardless, I leaped to find meaning in its visit. Wikipedia at hand, I learned that "peregrine" comes from the Latin word for "wanderer." That was perfect; my own career has found me wandering. This potential new gig would entail additional wandering. It's a positive sign, I imagined. The peregrine is signaling that this is the right move; that the time is now; that I belong here awaiting a ninety-minute interview. How could the peregrine be wrong? But the Latin translation alone is not enough. I next discovered that the peregrine is an "animal totem that brings higher wisdom and greater knowledge to deal with personal dilemmas." That's the mother lode of omen evidence. This new position, I reasoned, is meant to be—predestined, a foregone conclusion.

I watched the falcon off and on for more than an hour, convinced that I was reading the message correctly. Eventually as I watched, the bird looked away and—with wings open—slipped gracefully from the ledge. It dipped below my line of sight, and did not reappear. I felt blessed to receive and interpret the powerful totem. Truthfully, I sensed greater blessing and pleasure having simply been there to see the peregrine up close and personal. I knew the species had adapted to urban high-rise life, and had acquired a taste for European pigeon cuisine—fresh off the wing. Perhaps a pigeon below had prompted the bird to leave me behind.

I appreciated my interview. There is no better way than preparing for such an interview to learn at depth about another institution. Seventeen members of that university's committed community grilled me, but not unpleasantly. I answered questions as well as I could. Not once did I think, "Oh God, why did I answer it that way? I could have done so much better." I even found a way to work the falcon into a response. Perhaps that is why the following week the search firm called to say, "Thanks, but no thanks."

I accepted that notification with sincere relief. Judy was right about the position at that point in our lives. By then, I had even reinterpreted the peregrine sighting. The falcon did not appear to me in its regal form, an exquisite work of art. For goodness sakes, the bird presented itself with ruffled feathers, wind-whipped and battered. It appeared in an act of escape: seeking shelter from the morning's unpleasant, tumultuous conditions. Perhaps that is why I appeared in Atlanta that morning, seeking shelter from some unpleasant weather. Maybe the bird employed its own poor judgment when it lifted from its overnight perch, and found itself tossed in stormy skies until the building offered refuge.

I misread the wind-bludgeoned bird, seeing only a positive interpretation. I reached the wrong conclusion. The peregrine carried a message I failed to see, expressing instead, "Beware of these wanderings, especially given the conditions that prevail within your decision framework." The bird was saying, "Look at me. See how foolish I have been. I ventured forth this morning when I should have stayed home. I'm fortunate to have found shelter."

In all honesty, I do not normally look for premonitions from nature. Instead, I seek lessons from nature. Obviously, the peregrine did not signal an interview outcome. Instead, the bird prompted me to think deeply. Like the falcon, I had ventured out during a period of less than favorable conditions. I was casting for another position that would have been akin to finding temporary respite from ill winds on a precarious perch seventeen stories high in the torrent. I was looking to escape something, and not consciously reaching with positive purpose. Escaping is only part of completing the equation. A purposeful journey takes us to something, not just away. I violated that cardinal rule of career rationality. My mother used to caution us, "Be careful what you wish for; you just might get it."

I still ponder that recent juncture in my life. Had they offered me a finalist interview on-campus, would I have gone? I think my relief suggests that I had already made up my mind. But they did not test or tempt me with an invitation. Nor had I called to withdraw my candidacy before they rejected me. Even with the benefit of a long look backward, I am still not entirely sure whether I would have gone through with a campus interview. Perhaps I do not need to know how I would have responded. We all have second-guessed other people's decisions. Here I am questioning my own decision—ironically, one I never had the chance to make. Leadership is about examining self, and learning from it. Looking back is a natural part of that essential introspection, so long as we focus mainly on what lies ahead. As with all other major decisions along the way, I am not wishing for a redo.

I reminded myself that mine had not been a life and death decision; it turned out not to be a decision at all. In contrast, a peregrine may not get a second chance to make up for poor judgment. I lost nothing from venturing to Atlanta for a rich learning experience. Sure, I invested a few days in preparing for the interview, and in traveling to and from. The key word is "invested." The trip paid dividends in understanding another university, meeting some very impressive people, and in knowing myself better. Interestingly, as a hopeful candidate I found promise in nature's totem; as a rejected semi-finalist, I found comfort in a different interpretation of that same animal sign. That alone served to remind me that nature often furnishes varying frames of reference, and an interpretation filter for our choosing.

So, what was my nature based leadership lesson? I puzzle a bit over whether NBL is best characterized as employing lessons drawn from nature. This discussion of totems and talismans, I believe, adds credence to the alternative (or complementary) notion that NBL is more about deriving lessons inspired by nature. Perhaps that distinction is not important. It is nature, in either case, that spurs the thinking that enriches our daily living, learning, serving, and leading. Think how dull my four-hour wait could have been. Consider what stimuli I would have missed had I simply looked out the window to see a bird on a ledge, and nothing more. Contemplate how uninspiring the trip would have been if I had not paid attention to the retreating storm and the howling winds it brought to Atlanta on its backside.

Nature based leadership, as I preach to anyone who will listen, enables and inspires us to pay attention, to actually look hard at what surrounds us every minute of every day. Unless we look, we will not see. We will especially not see what everyday blindness to our world hides from far too many, even when in plain sight. And unless we truly see, life and living will never evoke feelings deeply enough to spur us to action. Action, which in the 1859 words of Antioch's founding president Horace Mann, leads to making a difference for today and tomorrow, that winning of some "victory for humanity."

Nature is a lens through which I view all that life comprises. Nature nurtures my soul, enriches my mind, commands my heart, fuels my body, and lifts my spirit. I enjoyed toying with the idea of a peregrine falcon as my talisman, my totem. Most importantly, I found solace that this daring bird of prey, this thing of wild beauty, this symbol of nature's fury and mastery, had alighted on a seventeenth story ledge during that brief period when I was wrestling with a personal and professional dilemma, and at a time when a mid-Atlantic coastal storm had ushered some rough weather into the Southland. The mix allowed me to look deeply into urban wildness and its temporal intersection with my life and my inner self. I see more clearly through the filter and magnification of nature's lenses. I am grateful for every opportunity I have to look, see, feel, and act. A lesson in nature, or one inspired by nature? I accept either, with deep appreciation for yet another chance to experience, learn, and grow.

Stephen B. Jones Bio

Now 43 years beyond his bachelor's degree in forestry, Steve is devoting his life to championing the cause of Nature-Inspired Learning and Leading. He created the emerging field of nature based leadership (NBL), founding the NBL Institute at Antioch University New England while serving as that institution's president, his third university presidency, and eighth university. He preceded his 32 years in higher education with a dozen years in the paper and allied products manufacturing industry, where among other assignments he conducted tree nutrition and forest fertilization research for four years and served another two years in the Corporate Office of Environmental Affairs. He holds a doctoral degree in Natural Resources Management and has done scholarly work in the human dimensions of forest resource management. He is president and CEO of Great Blue Heron consulting, and is writing extensively on NBL and Nature-Inspired Learning and Leading. Steve and Judy (wife since June 1972) reside in the Tennessee Valley region of northern Alabama.

Cheryl Charles Bio, Author of the Foreword

Cheryl Charles, Ph.D., is an innovator, author, organizational executive, and educator. In 2015, Cheryl was named Research Scholar and founding Executive Director of the Nature Based Leadership Institute at Antioch University New England. The institute envisions a world in which all humans live, learn, serve, and lead in healthy balance with the natural world; it applies nature's lessons to achieve economic, environmental, and social justice. Cheryl is the co-founder, president, and CEO Emerita of the Children & Nature Network (www.childrenandnature.org). She coordinates the network's international activities and participates as a member of the Science of Nature-Based Learning Collaborative Research Network, a three-year project funded by the National Science Foundation. Recipient of numerous awards for her leadership, she served as founding National Director of the pioneering K-12, interdisciplinary environmental education programs, Project Learning Tree and Project WILD, which remain available and widely used. Author Mark Gerzon named Cheryl a "new patriot" for her pioneering work to bring ecological concepts into mainstream schooling.

TEALarbor stories
The Ecology & Art of Listening

TEALarbor stories' mission is to compassionately support people as they discover & convey through writing their deepest stories.

...using nature-based and creative processes for guidance through writing, nature, & life's difficult landscapes...

Writing Services
Consultations, Mentorship, Editing, Proofreading, Copywriting

Story & Nature Guiding©
Nature experiences for healing and insight

Life Transition Support
Practices for thriving during significant change, grief, loss

Mediated Conversations
Environmental Disputes, Family Disputes, Conflict Coaching, Facilitated Conversations

...offering individual guidance, small and large group workshops, presentations, retreats, trainings, courses...

Contact

Founder:	Jennifer J. Wilhoit, Ph.D.
Email:	tealarborstories@gmail.com
Website:	www.tealarborstories.com
Blog:	tealarborstories.blogspot.com
LinkedIn:	www.linkedin.com/in/jenniferjwilhoit
Facebook:	www.facebook.com/tealarborstories/
Twitter:	twitter.com/TEALarbor
Amazon:	www.amazon.com/Jennifer-J.-Wilhoit/e/B005SWWIPK

Great Blue Heron, LLC

Great Blue Heron understands that every lesson for living, learning, serving, and leading is either written indelibly *in*, or is compellingly inspired *by* nature. My ultimate intent is to enhance life and enterprise success, even as we together (you and GBH) sow the seeds for responsible Earth stewardship.

GBH strives to assist clients to:

- LOOK more closely
- SEE more completely
- FEEL deeply
- ACT with conviction and purpose

Great Blue Heron, LLC is purpose-driven, passion-fueled, and dedicated to changing lives and enterprises. I am president and CEO. A nature-enthusiast and grateful Earth citizen, I am GBH's lead scholar, principal author, primary consultant, and designated speaker.

Contact:

Great Blue Heron, LLC
213 Legendwood Drive NW
Madison, AL 35757
steve.jones.0524@gmail.com

Watch for a soon-to-be-launched Great Blue Heron website!

ABOUT THE AUTHOR

 Steve created the emerging field of nature-based leadership (NBL), founding the NBL Institute at Antioch University New England while serving as that institution's president— his third university presidency and eighth university. He preceded his thirty-two years in higher education with a dozen years in the paper and allied-products manufacturing industry where, among other assignments, he conducted tree-nutrition and forest-fertilization research for four years and served another two years in the Corporate Office of Environmental Affairs. As Alabama region land manager in 1981–84, he oversaw operations on the company's five hundred square miles of forestland across twenty-seven Alabama counties. He has a bachelor's degree in forestry and a doctorate in natural resources management. Steve and Judy (his wife since June 1972) reside in the Tennessee Valley region of northern Alabama. Steve's ultimate intent is to enhance lives and enterprise success, even as he sows the seeds for responsible earth stewardship.

Made in the USA
Middletown, DE
25 January 2017